D1529955

THE
FRESHWATER
FISH
I D E N T I F I E R

THE
FRESHWATER
FISH
IDENTIFIER

SCOTT WEIDENSAUL

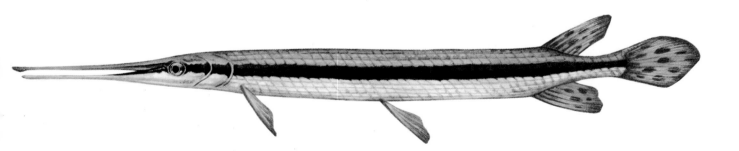

MALLARD
PRESS

MALLARD PRESS

An imprint of BDD Promotional
Book Company, Inc.
666 Fifth Avenue, New York, NY 10103

Mallard Press and its accompanying design and
logo are trademarks of BDD Promotional Book
Company, Inc.

First published in the United States of America
in 1992 by the Mallard Press

ISBN 0–7924–5576–2

This book was designed and produced by
Quintet Publishing Limited
6 Blundell Street
London N7 9BH

Creative Director: Terry Jeavons
Designer: Chris Dymond, Peter Radcliffe
Project Editor: Judith Simons
Picture Researcher: Scott Weidensaul
Illustrator: Andrew Tewson

Typeset in Great Britain by
Central Southern Typesetters, Eastbourne
Manufactured in Hong Kong by
Regent Publishing Services Limited
Printed in Hong Kong by
Leefung-Asco Printers Limited

Contents

Introduction

The bobber twitches, then pauses. Another jiggle, then it dances across the water, throwing up a wake that sparkles in the sun. The angler sets the hook, and a few moments later a fish is flopping in the net.

But what fish? Most fishermen, even those who are ardent about their sport, recognize only the most popular gamefish. At that, many lump related species together, not bothering to differentiate between black and white crappies, spotted and largemouth bass, pike and pickerel – to say nothing of the larger, more confusing groups such as sunfish and catfish, or the myriad varieties of minnows.

Knowing what fish are in your favorite waters fulfills two purposes – it makes you a more knowledgeable outdoorsman, more appreciative of the impressive diversity of natural systems, and it helps on a practical level, since knowing what fish are present, along with an awareness of their habits, ultimately puts more fish on the stringer.

This book is an identification guide, covering more than 90 of North America's most common and widespread freshwater fish, including virtually all game species, and many of the significant bait and rough fish that an angler will encounter.

Fish identification is somewhat different from identifying birds, which usually have

OPPOSITE Knowing the habits and habitat of the fish you seek will ultimately put more on the stringer. In a fast-moving lowland stream like this, smallmouth bass and brown trout would be likely.

BELOW Spray flies from a fisherman's reel as he casts in the morning light for pike.

bold colors and distinctive patterns. So do some fish, but with many the characteristic points are much more subtle – the number of rays in the fins, for example. Many scientific identification keys for fish rely on such methods as counting the number of scales along the lateral line, techniques which, while extremely accurate, are more time-consuming and difficult than most sport anglers desire. Wherever possible, the fish included here are identified by the unique sum of their parts – color, pattern, and shape. Range information is also included, and should be a first step in making an identification; if you think you've caught a Dolly Varden, but you pulled it out of a stream in North Carolina, you had better think again.

Habitat

It may be that water is always two hydrogen atoms bonded to one of oxygen, but as with so much in nature context is everything, and a cold mountain stream is vastly different from a warm, silty farm pond. Differences in habitats exert a profound influence on what species of fish are found in which waters, since every variety has its own special needs.

A creek, for example, may change dramatically as it flows over its miles of streambed. Starting life as a snow melt or run-off stream in the mountains, it will be shaded by overhanging trees, flow very cold and fast and will be full of dissolved oxygen. However, the water is probably rather sterile,

BELOW Habitat exerts a profound influence on what species of fish are found in any given area. Mountain streams, with their cold water and low fertility, are home to brook trout, redbelly daces, and others that cannot tolerate warm, silty water.

since most creeks flow over barren rock – the so-called freestone streams. Such rapid, or high-gradient, streams support species like redbelly daces, brook trout, and darters that require low temperatures and exceptionally pure water.

The fish do not live in a vacuum; the minnows and trout are only part of a web interlocking all the living organisms and non-living aspects of the stream. Vastly complex even in a tiny freestone stream, the web begins with inorganic components – air, water, mineral nutrients, and solar energy, which are used by green plants that photosynthesize food within their cells. The plants, in turn, support invertebrates like aquatic insect larvae, copepods, and others; these are in their turn food for larger predators like crayfish, bigger insects, and fish. The chain careens from animal to animal, reaching beyond the boundaries of the stream as mink catch trout and grasshoppers tumble to the water.

As the stream moves from the mountains, its waters begin to slow. Fields and pastures allow sunlight to warm the water, and runoff that carries silt may make the formerly crystal waters turbid. In quiet pools, the bottom is not gravel but mud, and emergent plants like pickerelweed crowd the shallow edges. In summer, the water temperature may climb too high for heat-sensitive species like brook trout, but not for more tolerant fish like creek chubs, brown trout and bluntnose minnows. There is a change, as well, in the invertebrate life, with more mud-dwelling species like burrowing mayflies, and fewer cold-water types like riffle penny beetles.

And so the changes go, from habitat to habitat. Deep, northern lakes support different fish (walleye, pike, yellow perch) than shallower lakes of the Midwest and South (largemouth bass, bluegills, brown bullheads). Some species are adapted to only one particular habitat: the sauger is found only in large bodies of water, while the almost identical walleye may be found in lakes both large and small, as well as rivers, and even big streams.

Life Histories

Most fish have definite spawning seasons, the timing of which is controlled by such factors as water temperature and, especially, the ratio of daylight to darkness, known as the photoperiod.

Spawning behavior varies widely, from the almost random to the exceedingly precise. The female golden shiner simply scatters her eggs over beds of aquatic plants, while attending males fertilize them as they drop. The male sticklebacks, however, construct elaborate nests of woven grass that form ball-sized globes, with an entrance tunnel through the middle. The female is enticed inside, where she lays her eggs.

The male stickleback defends his nest, eggs, and young, a common behavior among many fish. Anglers know that male sunfish and bass are at their most aggressive in the spring and early summer, when they are defending the large, plate-sized depressions in shallow water where their mate's eggs have been laid. The males will attack almost anything that enters the vicinity of the nest, making them so easy to catch that many states close the bass season during the breeding season.

ABOVE In its red-and-green breeding colors, this male chum salmon plucked a fly from an Alaskan river, even though Pacific salmon do not eat during their spawning run. The instinct to attack, however, seems strong despite the lack of hunger.

OPPOSITE **Fisheries biologists use electroshocking devices to temporarily stun fish, allowing easy sampling of streams and lakes.**

lakes up tributary rivers. One fish, the American eel, reverses the usual procedure by maturing in freshwater but returning to the ocean to breed.

Parental care by fish is rudimentary: in most species the eggs are simply abandoned after laying, and even among those that care for the eggs and fry, the attention lasts only for a few weeks. The fry are capable of feeding themselves from hatching (or, in the case of the few species of live-bearers, from birth), and their parents and older relatives may well be their worst enemies, since predaceous fish have no qualms about eating the young of their own species.

Conservation

Any discussion of fish must include a word about conservation. North America's waterways are under increasing pressure from human use and abuse. Despite toughened environmental laws against "point" pollutants like toxic effluents, the toll of "nonpoint" pollutants like agricultural and sewage run-off, sedimentation, and road salt continues to grow. In many parts of the continent, acid deposition in the form of acidic rain, snow, and fog is an all but unchecked menace that has rendered many lakes and streams sterile.

Anglers should be among the forefront of those working for a cleaner, healthier environment. Such an attitude is expressed in more than just support for conservation causes, however – it must be part of one's conduct in day to day life. Water conservation in the home, an avoidance of lawn care and garden chemicals (which eventually find their way into local waterways) and maintenance of home sewage systems, for instance, are equally important. So is a judicious approach to fishing. Many anglers have adopted a catch-and-release policy, and under no circumstances should anyone keep more fish than they can reasonably use.

North America's fisheries are a valuable, renewable resource – but only if they are cared for properly.

ABOVE **Scooped high, an American shad's upriver migration takes an abrupt turn for the worse after it fell for a brightly colored dart. It is an anadromous fish native to the East.**

Spawning is a long-distance undertaking for many fish. The best-known examples are the anadromous salmon, which ascend their natal rivers after years at sea; the Pacific salmon species, with one exception, die after breeding. But salmon are not the only fish that make long spawning runs. Many others, including American shad, striped bass, smelt, and sturgeons, enter freshwater to breed, and other landlocked species like walleye, white suckers, trout, and lake whitefish make spawning runs from large

Families of North American Freshwater Fish

In the hierarchy of classification, families are units into which are grouped those species with general similarities, but which exhibit substantial variation from one to the next.

In all, more than 35 families are represented in North America's freshwaters, with members of still more families entering from the ocean on occasion. The 20 families that follow (they are given expanded treatment in the species accounts section of this book) are among the most important.

In scientific nomenclature, animal family names end in -idae, and are (like all scientific names) based on the dead languages of Greek and Latin. Within each family are genera, which are smaller groups of more closely allied organisms, and within each genus are the individual species belonging to the group. Each species has a two-word scientific name: the first, which is capitalized, is the genus name, shared by the animal's closest relatives, and the second is the specific name. The combination of genus and specific name is unique to each living thing, and allows recognition across global language barriers.

Petromyzontidae – Lampreys

Primitive, cartilaginous skeleton; round, jawless mouth with horny teeth; eel-like shape. Larvae (ammocoetes) are blind.

Acipenseridae – Sturgeons

Large, primitive-looking fish with bony plates running the length of the body. Small, sucker mouth on underside of prominent snout, with small barbels at front edge of mouth.

Polyodontidae – Paddlefish

Single species in North America; large fish with snout that forms wide, thin paddle nearly one-half of body length.

Lepisosteidae – Gars

Long, thin fish with narrow, tooth-studded snout; dorsal fin set far back above anal fin; body covered with ganoid scales. Can breathe air with specialized swim bladder.

Amiidae – Bowfins

Bony head; long, sinuous dorsal fin, and rounded caudal fin; tube-like body.

Anguillidae – Freshwater eels

Long, snaky body; dorsal, caudal, and anal fins continuous. Catadromous, spawning in Sargasso Sea.

Clupeidae – Herrings

Body deeply compressed; large anal fin and dorsal fin set far to rear; mouth large, with jutting lower jaw. No lateral line; belly has saw-toothed edge. Many species anadromous.

Salmonidae – Trout, salmon, and whitefishes

Streamlined shape; adipose fin; axillary process at base of pelvic fins. Many species anadromous, some undergoing dramatic physical changes after entering freshwater.

Osmeridae – Smelts

Small, streamlined fish resembling trout; adipose fin but no axillary process at base of pelvic fins. Some species anadromous.

Esocidae – Pikes

Jaws toothy, large and wide, projecting forward to form a duck-bill mouth; body streamlined; dorsal and anal fins set far back.

Cyprinidae – Minnows

Large family, with more than 200 species in North America. Most, but not all, under 1 ft/30 cm in length. No adipose fin; no teeth in jaws.

Catostomidae – Suckers

Bottom-feeders; mouth adapted into sucker shape (less pronounced in some species), lips thick, jaws toothless. No adipose fin; soft rays in dorsal fin usually 10 or more.

Ictaluridae – Freshwater catfishes

Four pairs of barbels surrounding mouth. Adipose fin present; pectoral and dorsal fins have hard rays forming spines. Some species have venom glands at base of spines.

Atherinidae – Silversides

Small, thin, streamlined fish with two separated dorsal fins; single spines each on second dorsal, anal, pectoral fins. Snout flattened, lower jaw jutting.

Gasterosteidae – Sticklebacks

Pelvic fin consists of single spine; free spines along back anterior to soft dorsal fin. Caudal peduncle very narrow.

Percichthyidae – Temperate basses

Prominent spines on opercle; two dorsal fins separate or nearly so; complete lateral line.

Centrarchidae – Sunfishes

No opercle spine, but opercular flap well developed and often colorful. Dorsal fins joined; three or more spines in anal fin.

Percidae – Perches

Separate dorsal fins; one or two anal spines. Darters are bottom-dwelling fish, other members of family free-swimming.

Sciaenidae – Drums

Mostly marine, with one freshwater member. Dorsal fin joined with distinct notch; anal fin with two spines, second spine long and flattened.

Cottidae – Sculpins

Large head tapering to narrow body. Anal fin without spines; pectoral fins large and fan-like.

Daybreak is one of the best
times for fishing, especially for light-sensitive
species like walleye that will retreat to deeper
waters as the sun climbs.

Species Accounts

NOTE

All-tackle world record information has been provided for key game species, and is printed courtesy of the International Game Fish Association, Fort Lauderdale, Florida. The imperial measurements provided are exactly as supplied; the metric equivalents are the nearest approximations.

FAMILY PETROMYZONTIDAE

There are several closely related species of brook lampreys in North America, difficult for any but the expert to sort out. All are fairly small, under 1 ft/30 cm in length, with a long, eel-like body, a dorsal fin that may be divided into two lobes in some species, and a sucker-disk mouth filled with horny, rasping growths that resemble teeth.

Unlike the better-known sea lamprey, brook lampreys are not predaceous. For the first four or five years of life the larvae, known as ammocoetes, live in U-shaped

Brook lamprey

Icthyomyzon and *Lampetra* spp.

Average length: Under 1 ft/30 cm.

Habitat: Streams, rivers.

Habits: Larvae burrow in stream bottom.

burrows in muddy stream bottoms, blindly scavenging for food. They eventually metamorphose from the larval stage into adulthood, developing the sucker-disk and eyes, and living just long enough to breed.

The American brook lamprey (*Lampetra lamottei*), one of the most widespread species, is found in streams and rivers from the southern Appalachians to Quebec and west to Canada. Like most brook lampreys it is brown, and reaches a length of about 6 in/15 cm.

Easily one of the most despised fish in North America, the sea lamprey has had a significant impact on the Great Lakes fishery since it moved from Lake Ontario to the rest of the chain. The opening of the Welland Canal in 1833 gave the lamprey a way around Niagara Falls, and within a century caused a 97 percent drop in gamefish catches, especially lake trout.

The lamprey, a jawless predator with a cartilage skeleton, is one of the most primitive fish in the world. It swims up to other fish and latches on with its suction mouth,

Sea lamprey

Petromyzon marinus

Average length: Under 3 ft/90 cm.

Habitat: Lakes, rivers.

Habits: Anadromous; feeds on other fish.

using its rasping teeth to tear a hole in the side or belly, then feeds on blood and body fluids. The wounds may kill the victim directly, or it may succumb to infection, although many fish survive.

The sea lamprey reaches a length of 3 ft/ 90 cm. A two-lobed dorsal fin merges with the tail, and small pectoral fins are present behind the seven gill openings; the base color is olive-brown with darker brown mottling. In addition to the landlocked populations, sea lampreys are also anadromous along the entire East coast.

FAMILY ACIPENSERIDAE

Lake sturgeon

Acipenser fulvescens

DATA

Average weight: 50 lb/23 kg.

Length range: 5–7 ft/1.5–2.1 m.

Fishing tackle: Heavy gear; cut or live bait.

Habitat: Lakes, rivers.

Habits: Bottom-feeder.

A victim of overzealous fishing, the lake sturgeon is a threatened species over most of its North American range, which stretches from Hudson Bay and Alberta to Pennsylvania and the lower Mississippi Valley. It has been completely wiped out in some areas.

Once an important commercial species, the lake sturgeon grows to astounding sizes – sturgeons of more than 6 ft/1.8 m and 200 lb/91 kg were once routine, and the largest ever caught weighed more than 300 lb/136 kg. In cold northern waters it takes years to achieve such weights; one 200-lb/91-kg sturgeon from Ontario was found to be 154 years old.

The lake sturgeon is usually brownish and heavily armored, with plates on the head, and rows of horny scutes along the spine and both sides of the body. The nose is extremely long and pointed, but the mouth is set far back and under the head, just behind a set of long barbules.

Atlantic sturgeon

Acipenser oxyrhynchus

DATA

Average weight: 150 lb/68 kg.

Maximum length: 12 ft/3.6 m.

Fishing tackle: Heavy tackle; cut bait.

Habitat: Rivers.

Habits: Anadromous; bottom-feeder.

The Atlantic sturgeon is North America's freshwater giant, reaching lengths of 10 ft/ 3 m with a few monsters of 18 ft/5.5 m known from the 19th century.

Unlike the lake sturgeon, the Atlantic is anadromous, ascending rivers from Canada to the Carolinas to spawn in spring. Unfortunately, dams, pollution, and overfishing have seriously hurt the abundance and size of the population, and it is today protected over most of its range.

Like all sturgeons, the Atlantic has a primitive appearance accentuated by the rows of body scutes and an underslung, sucker mouth that allows them to feed on the bottom. They are extremely slow-growing fish, not reaching maturity until about age 15, and living for up to 75 years. A mature female is capable of laying upwards of 2½ million eggs each spawning season; the young sturgeons spend three or four years in freshwater before descending to the sea to grow to adulthood.

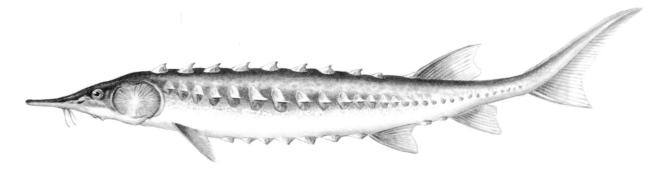

White sturgeon

Acipenser transmontanus

DATA

Average weight: 500 lb/227 kg.

Maximum length: 12 ft/3.6 m.

Fishing tackle: Heavy gear; cut bait or crustaceans.

Habitat: Rivers.

Habits: Anadromous; bottom-feeder.

Second in size only to the Atlantic sturgeon, the white sturgeon of western coastal rivers is a behemoth, growing to more than 8 ft/ 2.4 m in length, and weighing more than 1,800 lb/816 kg.

As its name suggests, the white sturgeon is a pale, silvery color, but is otherwise similar in appearance to other sturgeons. The only other western sturgeon, the green, rarely exceeds 2 ft/60 cm in length, has a strongly pointed snout and is dark olive in color. The green sturgeon is found in river mouths from San Francisco to Alaska.

Because its flesh is excellent, the white sturgeon was overfished commercially, and populations have suffered in many areas; dam-building has also taken a toll. But protection has stabilized sturgeon numbers in most rivers, and its value as a rod-and-reel gamefish is now recognized – the effect of hooking one has been likened to snagging a truck.

The white sturgeon is found in rivers from southern California to Alaska, and there are also some landlocked populations in the Columbia drainage.

FAMILY POLYODONTIDAE

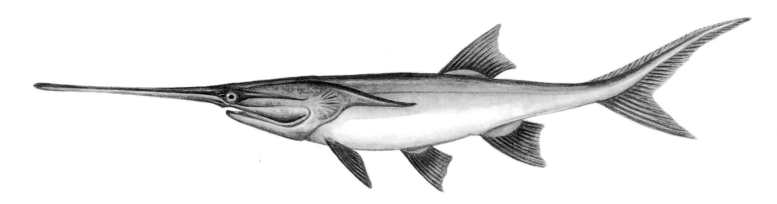

Paddlefish

Polyodon spathula

DATA

Average weight: 40–90 lb/18–41 kg.

Maximum length: 8 ft/2.4 m.

Fishing tackle: Heavy snagging gear.

Habitat: Rivers.

Habits: Plankton-eater; migratory.

The paddlefish wins the prize, hands-down, for oddest-looking North American fish. A relict of an ancient family (the only other member is found in China), it is unmistakable thanks to its bizarre, spoonbill snout.

Paddlefish are filter feeders, swimming through the water with their huge mouths agape; water passes over fine gill rakers that net minute crustaceans and other varieties of plankton. Despite its almost microscopic diet, there is nothing diminutive about the paddlefish, which can grow to 8 ft/2.4 m and more than 200 lb/91 kg.

In profile, a paddlefish has a streamlined form, with a sharply forked tail and a dorsal fin set far back on the spine; the gill covers come to a long point. Young paddlefish hatch with no paddle, but the unique snout begins to develop in about three weeks. The exact purpose of the proboscis is unclear, but presumably helps the fish maintain an even keel while feeding.

Paddlefish are found in the Mississippi, Missouri, and Ohio drainages, in both rivers and lakes.

FAMILY LEPISOSTEIDAE

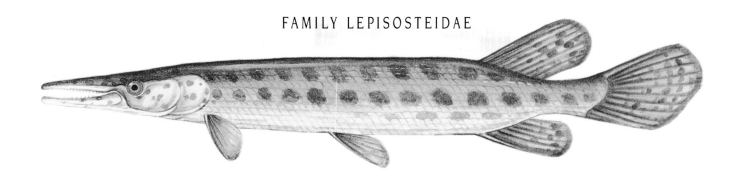

Spotted gar

Lepisosteus oculatus

DATA

Average length: 4 ft/1.2 m.

Fishing tackle: Medium gear; live bait or lures.

Habitat: Lakes, rivers.

Habits: Fish-eater.

Gars are considered primitive fish for a number of reasons. Much of their skeleton is composed of cartilage rather than bone, their heads carry heavy, bony plates, and they are covered with small, hard ganoid scales, which do not overlap like the scales of more advanced fish.

The spotted gar is a mid-sized species, attaining a length of about 4 ft/1.2 m. It is a long, slim fish vaguely resembling a pike, with a long snout studded with sharp teeth. The base color is greenish, with large, dark spots on the body and tail. The six species of eastern gars are quite similar; the spotted gar is best identified by the large, round spots on the top of the head, while the closely related Florida gar of the Southeast lacks the spots, and has a shorter, heavier snout.

Gars inhabit warm lakes and sluggish rivers, and feed primarily on fish. The spotted gar is found from the Great Lakes in the North, and southward to northwest Florida and Texas.

Longnose gar

Lepisosteus osseus

DATA

Average length: 4–5 ft/1.2–1.5 m.

Fishing tackle: Medium gear; live bait or plugs.

Habitat: Lakes, rivers.

Habits: Fish-eater.

The most widespread of North America's gars, the longnose gar carries the family's propensity for slimness to its greatest extreme with a tube-like body and a needle-like nose.

The longnose is found from Quebec to Montana and south to Texas in lakes and slow-moving rivers. It may grow to 5 ft/1.5 m in length, olive on the back and lighter below, with a few scattered, large spots toward the tail. If in doubt, measure the length of the snout; if it is more than twice the distance from the corner of the mouth to the edge of the gill flap, the fish is a longnose gar.

Gars can be very common within their range – a combination of low fishing pressure, abundant food, and eggs which are poisonous to mammals and birds that would otherwise eat them.

The shortnose gar is the "Plain Jane" of the genus *Lepisosteus*, lacking the attractive markings of the spotted and Florida gars. A widespread fish, it is found through the Mississippi River system, the Great Lakes, and as far south as the southern Plains, although it is not as abundant in the north as other gar species.

Shortnose gars are a dull brownish or olive color, with a few distinct small spots on the fins, but none on the body – or on top of the head, separating it easily from the

Shortnose gar

Lepisosteus platostomus

DATA

Average length: 4 ft/1.2 m.

Fishing tackle: Medium to heavy; live bait or lures.

Habitat: Slow rivers, lakes.

Habits: Drifts quietly near surface.

spotted gar, even when one is glimpsed finning near the surface of the water.

None of the gars are considered prime sport fish, although they are more popular in some areas than in others. Like all gars, the shortnose has a modified swim bladder that removes oxygen from air – a very primitive "lung" that permits the gars to survive where stale water would kill other species.

Reaching lengths of 12 ft/3.6 m and weights of more than 100 lb/45 kg, and carrying a mouth studded with teeth, the alligator gar is one of the most imposing fish in freshwater – and it is little wonder that those who fish for these monsters often carry a gun to subdue the gar before it is boated. There are even unconfirmed reports of attacks on humans.

The alligator gar is primarily southern, found in quiet backwaters and sluggish rivers along the Gulf Coast and up the

Alligator gar

Lepisosteus spathula

DATA

Maximum length: To 12 ft/3.6 m.

Fishing tackle: Heavy gear; wire leaders; live bait.

Habitat: Large rivers.

Habits: Ambushes fish.

Mississippi as far as Missouri. The coloration is usually a blend of brown and olive, like most gars, with dark blotches along the sides; the snout is short and rather broad, giving an impression of contained strength.

Gars feed largely on fish, which are located by sight and carefully stalked, or allowed to come within ambush range. The gar's hunting technique is usually to rest near the surface, motionless, trying as much as possible to look like an innocent log. It often works.

FAMILY AMIIDAE

Bowfin

Amia calva

> **DATA**
>
> **Average weight:** 5–6 lb/2.3–2.7 kg.
>
> **Average length:** 2 ft/60 cm.
>
> **Fishing tackle:** Medium spinning or casting gear; live bait or lures.
>
> **Habitat:** Lakes, rivers.
>
> **Habits:** Extremely strong fighter.

A fisherman who catches his first bowfin, not knowing what it is, can be forgiven for thinking he's caught a prehistoric throwback – for in a sense he has. The bowfin belongs to an ancient family of fish, once more common (judging from the fossil record) but now claiming just this species.

Like the gars, bowfins have a cartilaginous skeleton, and a head encased in bony plates – much the same body plan followed by primitive fish for millions of years. The body is long and tube-shaped, with a sinuous dorsal fin that stretches almost to the tail. During the breeding season the ventral fins become a bright aqua-green, and males year-round have a dark "eye" spot, ringed with yellow, at the base of the tail. Also like gars, bowfins have modified swim bladders, and can breathe air if the dissolved oxygen level of the water drops.

Bowfins are found across the eastern United States and southeastern Canada from Quebec to Florida, usually in lakes and slow-moving rivers. They reach a length of 2 ft/60 cm, and they are among the fiercest fighters in their range.

FAMILY ANGUILLIDAE

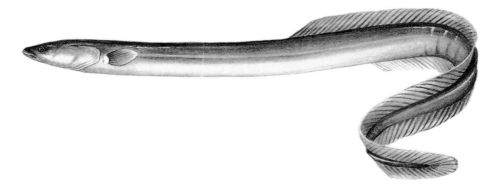

American eel

Anguilla rostrata

> **DATA**
>
> **Average length:** 3–4 ft/90–120 cm.
>
> **Fishing tackle:** Light or medium gear; live bait.
>
> **Habitat:** Rivers, streams.
>
> **Habits:** Catadromous; bottom-dwelling.

The American eel has one of the oddest life histories of any North American fish, linking the headwaters of eastern rivers with the deep waters of the Sargasso Sea off Bermuda.

Eels are catadromous – that is, they spawn in saltwater but live in fresh, the opposite of salmon. Eels from North America and Europe both use the giant, mid-ocean eddy known as the Sargasso Sea, with each female scattering up to 10 million tiny eggs. The eggs hatch into minute, leaf-shaped larvae known as leptocephala, which begin to migrate toward land – American eels going northwest, European eels east. By the time they reach the mouths of rivers they are known as elvers, and are about 6 in/15 cm long. Males stay near the river mouth, but females migrate to the headwaters; both sexes stay in freshwater for five to seven years, with the females attaining a length of about 4 ft/1.2 m. Males remain much smaller. When mature, both sexes return to the ocean, spawn and die.

Eels have a sweet, oily flesh that has been prized (more so in Europe) for centuries. Easily caught on bait and hard to remove from a hook, eels are often scorned by sport fishermen trying to catch other species.

FAMILY CLUPEIDAE

Alewife

Alosa pseudoharengus

DATA

Average length: 6–12 in/15–30 cm.

Habitat: Large lakes, rivers.

Habits: Anadromous; some populations landlocked.

The Welland Canal, which allowed the sea lamprey into the Great Lakes, also provided passage for the alewife, a small member of the herring family that makes spawning runs up the rivers of the Atlantic coast. Once in the Great Lakes, the alewife quickly adapted to a landlocked existence, and is now one of the most common bait fish in the lakes. In fact, it has overpopulated some portions of the lakes, and massive summer die-offs, and competition with native species, have been a problem ever since.

Alewives are built on the standard herring plan, with a deeply compressed body, forked tail, and bright, silvery color. Sea-run alewives reach 1 ft/30 cm in length, while land-locked specimens rarely exceed half that. They are a commercially valuable species along the coast, and some sport fishermen take them, along with the similar blueback herring. From a sport perspective, the alewife's significance lies in its importance as a forage fish for the trout and salmon introduced into the Great Lakes.

American shad

Alosa sapidissima

DATA

Average weight: 4–5 lb/1.8–2.3 kg.

North American record: 11 lb 4 oz/ 5.1 kg; Connecticut River, Massachusetts, 1986.

Fishing tackle: Medium spinning or fly gear; bright-colored darts and flies.

Habitat: Rivers.

Habits: Anadromous.

For the angler lucky enough to live near a shad river, the spring run of these large herring is a time for understandable excitement, for the American shad is unexcelled as a gamefish. Hooked on light tackle, the shad will battle furiously, punctuating lightning runs with high, acrobatic leaps – and just when you think the fight is over, the shad roars off again, seemingly undaunted.

An anadromous species, the shad spawns in river headwaters but spends most of its life at sea. It is found naturally in undammed rivers from southern Canada to Florida, and has been introduced to areas along the Pacific coast; sadly, some rivers that used to support vast shad fisheries, like the Susquehanna, have lost their shad runs because of hydroelectric dams.

American shad are the biggest North American herring, with females ("roes") reaching 30 in/76 cm and weighing 4 to 8 lb/ 1.8 to 3.6 kg, and males ("bucks") a bit smaller. Shad are silvery, with several dark spots behind the opercle, and a large mouth lined with special gill rakers, which filter plankton from the water. They do not feed in freshwater, however, and yet they strike at darts and flies, which in any case do not at all resemble the minute organisms that normally make up their diet.

The American shad is the largest North American herring, and like its relatives has a deeply compressed body, forked tail, and large mouth for filtering plankton from the water.

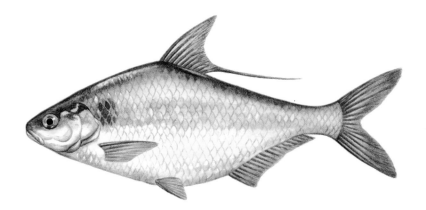

Gizzard shad

Dorosoma cepedianum

DATA

Average length: 1 ft/30 cm.

Habitat: Lakes.

Habits: Forms tight schools.

Not a sport fish, the gizzard shad is nevertheless crucial to angler success in many large lakes, where it is the prime forage species for striped bass and other game fish. Many anglers have learned to watch for boiling activity near the surface, which often indicates a gizzard shad school under attack by large, predatory fish. Casting live bait or a sinking lure through the school may bring a savage strike.

Gizzard shad are mid-size herrings, ranging in size from 6 to 18 in/15 to 46 cm, with a deep body and a long, threadlike ray at the base of the dorsal fin. They have a tremendous reproductive rate, and easily overpopulate a lake. This species is adapted to eating larger foods than its relatives, and will take prey up to the size of small crustaceans and aquatic insects, as well as freshwater plankton.

The very similar threadfin shad (D. *petenense*) is a southern species, widely stocked as a forage fish; it has a yellowish tail, and a clearly defined spot behind the opercle.

FAMILY SALMONIDAE

Lake whitefish

Coregonus clupeaformis

DATA

Average weight: 2–3 lb/900–1400 g.

Habitat: Lakes, rivers.

Habits: Insect-eater.

A valuable fish from both a sport and commercial perspective, the lake whitefish is found in cold, clean lakes from the Great Lakes basin and New England up into northern Canada.

Deep-bodied and silvery, the lake whitefish has a tiny, underslung mouth and a distinctively small head; the tail is forked. A large fish, it has been known to attain weights of 20 lb/9 kg, but overfishing, competition from introduced alewives, and the short northern growing season conspire to make the average lake whitefish about 1 ft/30 cm long, and weighing 2 to 3 lb/900 kg to 1400 g.

The diet consists largely of insects, copepods and small crustaceans. Lake whitefish gather in autumn at the mouths of tributary streams and rivers, which they ascend in a spawning run; in some lakes, spawning occurs in shallow shoals instead of moving water.

Pink salmon

Oncorhynchus gorbuscha

DATA

Average weight: 4 lb/1.8 kg.

Fishing tackle: Medium gear; bright lures.

Habitat: Rivers.

Habits: Anadromous.

More important to commercial fishermen than sport anglers, the pink salmon, or "humpback," is the smallest of the Pacific salmon, rarely growing larger than 8 or 9 lb/ 3.6 or 4.1 kg.

The pink is a two-year salmon, a species that matures in two years and returns to freshwater to breed. Like all salmon, it undergoes dramatic physical changes as it moves from the ocean to rivers; the male develops a pronounced back hump, and the hooklike snout that in salmon is known

as a kype, but unlike most salmon the color does not change, staying greenish-silver with dark, blotchy markings on the back and tail. The female retains her sea-run shape throughout the spawning cycle.

Pink salmon occur from the mid-California coast north to Alaska. In North America it makes up as much as a third of the total commercial salmon catch, while the Soviet Union, which also has pink salmon breeding on the Kamchatka Peninsula, relies on the species to an even greater extent.

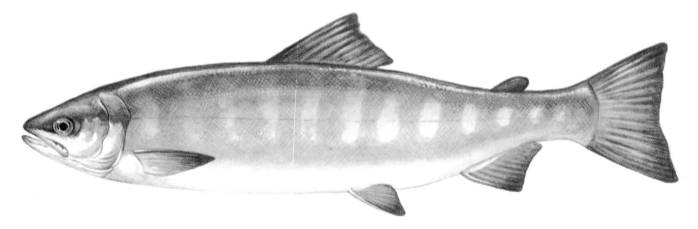

Chum salmon

Oncorhynchus keta

DATA

Average weight: 8–9 lb/3.6–4.1 kg.

Fishing tackle: Medium to heavy gear; bright lures.

Habitat: Rivers.

Habits: Anadromous.

Another salmon of only minor interest to sport anglers, the chum breeds along a wide swath of the north Pacific coast, from northern California to Alaska. The fall run of chum is the last of the year, and it is usually the heaviest on most rivers.

Known as dog salmon for the overgrown canine teeth of the spawning males, chum salmon males turn a dusky red in freshwater, with dark, vertical blotches. Chums average 8 or 9 lb/3.6 or 4.1 kg, with exceptional specimens exceeding 30 lb/14 kg.

Because chum salmon spawn so late in the year, they are an important food resource for many species of wildlife. On Alaska's Chilkat River, an exceptionally late chum run attracts thousands of bald eagles every winter, assuring them of food during a season when a full belly is usually anything but guaranteed.

While only the third most important commercial species in North America, the chum salmon accounts for nearly four-fifths of Japan's salmon fishery.

Coho salmon

Oncorhynchus kisutch

DATA

Average weight: 10 lb/4.5 kg.

North American record: 31 lb/14.1 kg; Cowichan Bay, British Columbia, 1947.

Fishing tackle: Medium to heavy spinning and fly gear; bright lures and flies.

Habitat: Rivers, lakes.

Habits: Anadromous.

The return of the "silvers," as coho are often known, is awaited with great expectation by sport anglers and commercial fishermen alike. Big, hard-fighting, and delicious, cohos are the epitome of Pacific salmon.

In its sea-going colors, the name silver is certainly appropriate: the coho is dark blue-black above shading to the color of burnished metal on its glittering sides. In breeding condition, it turns deep red, and the males develop hooked kypes. Cohos average 10 lb/4.5 kg, with weights to 25 or 30 lb/11 or 14 kg not unheard of.

The coho runs usually hit the mouths of the spawning rivers in midsummer, and the fish may fight their way hundreds of miles inland to spawn in the headwaters – that is, if hydroelectric dams, the bane of Pacific salmon, do not block their way. Coho are found right around the North Pacific rim, from California to Japan.

First introduced into the Great Lakes in the 1960s with spectacular results, coho now support a multimillion-dollar sport fishery. Sadly, many fish are contaminated with toxic metals and pesticides that have washed into the lakes, and experts caution against eating too many landlocked salmon.

Sockeye salmon

Oncorhynchus nerka

DATA

Average weight: 6 lb/2.7 kg.

Fishing tackle: Light to medium spinning gear.

Habitat: Rivers.

Habits: Anadromous.

The male sockeye salmon undergoes the most bizarre transformation of any Pacific salmon, as it moves from the ocean to its spawning grounds. What had been a slim, silver, streamlined fish turns quickly into a humpbacked monster, bright crimson, with a green head and a wickedly hooked mouth studded with teeth. The female also turns red and green, but retains her shape.

Sockeyes are, next to pinks, the smallest salmon, but their excellent flesh makes them the most highly prized by the fishing industry. Commercial fishermen annually land more sockeyes than any other species, taking them as they gather just offshore before making their upstream journey.

A landlocked form, the kokanee (O. *n. kennerlyi*), stays small, rarely growing bigger than 20 in/51 cm. A popular gamefish despite its size, the kokanee has been introduced as far east as Maine and Pennsylvania.

Chinook salmon

Oncorhynchus tshawytscha

The chinook, or king salmon, is the undisputed monarch of the Pacific rivers, reaching astonishing weights in excess of 125 lb/ 57 kg, making it the ultimate prize for the sport angler. Exceptionally long-lived, a chinook may take eight years to reach maturity, accounting in part for its great size.

It is an irony of nature that any of the salmon can be taken on sporting tackle during their spawning run, since they cease to feed once they reach freshwater. There are two reasons for the fasting: the shrinking digestive system makes way for the enlargement of the reproductive organs, and by not feeding, the salmon eliminate the chance of eating offspring from previous spawns, which may still be making their way to the ocean. Also, since the adult salmon all die following spawning, their fat reserves are sufficient to last them through the process.

Chinook salmon are found within the Pacific "salmon belt," from northern California to Alaska, and have been introduced to the Great Lakes. On some western rivers, notably the Columbia, there have traditionally been as many as three separate

DATA

Average weight: 22 lb/10 kg.

North American record: 97 lb 4 oz/ 44.1 kg; Kenai River, Alaska, 1985.

Fishing tackle: Heavy spinning or fly gear; spoons, spinners, flies.

Habitat: Rivers, lakes.

Habits: Anadromous.

RIGHT **Fresh and silver from the sea, chinook salmon are the biggest of the North American salmon, with records well in excess of 100 lb/45 kg. Once in freshwater to spawn, chinooks may take on a darker, cranberry hue.**

runs each year, staggered through the seasons. The chinook may travel hundreds, even thousands of miles upstream to spawn, using a keen sense of smell to trace their way back to the precise tributary where they, in turn, were hatched.

The chinook has dark spots on the back, dorsal fin, and tail. In lakes where coho and chinook both occur, anglers can separate the two similar species by looking at the mouth – the chinook has black gums at the base of the teeth, while the coho has a white line at the tooth base.

For years, the steelhead was considered merely a sea-run (or lake-run) form of the widespread rainbow trout. Recently, however, ichthyologists have decided that it is actually a salmon, and in 1989 reclassified it with the other members of the genus *Oncorhynchus*.

The steelhead is one of the premier sport fish in North America, packing tremendous power and stamina in a body that may weigh 25 or 30 lb/11 or 14 kg. Originally restricted to the rivers of the Pacific Northwest, steelhead have, like other salmon, been introduced to the Great Lakes, where they provide superior sport.

Steelhead

Oncorhynchus mykiss

DATA

Average weight: 9 lb/4.1 kg.

North American record: 42 lb 2 oz/ 19.1 kg; Bell Island, Alaska, 1970.

Fishing tackle: Medium to heavy fly or spinning gear; bright flies, spinners, spoons, plugs.

Habitat: Rivers, lakes.

Habits: Anadromous.

In the ocean (or lake), the steelhead is metallic silver with a dull gray head – hence the name. Once the fish matures and heads upstream to spawn, its color deepens, taking on the maroon lateral stripe of a rainbow trout that led to the confusion over classification. Unlike the other Pacific salmon, steelhead do not routinely die after spawning, although an old fish, stressed by the long, arduous process, is most likely to succumb at that time.

If the mountain whitefish were a little more brightly colored – and a shade less eager to take the fly – it might get the respect as a gamefish that it deserves. In the blue-ribbon trout streams of the Rocky Mountains, however, the whitefish is scorned by anglers seeking the cutthroats, browns, and rainbows that share its beautiful habitat.

Close kin of the trout and salmon, the mountain whitefish has the same graceful body and small adipose fin of its more esteemed relatives, but has a small, downturned, weak mouth that tears easily if

Mountain whitefish

Prosopium williamsoni

DATA

Average weight: 1–2 lb/450–900 g.

Fishing tackle: Light fly or spinning gear; wets, dries, nymphs, tiny lures.

Habitat: Streams, rivers.

Habits: Lifestyle similar to trout.

hooked. Nevertheless it is a scrappy fighter on light tackle or fly rod, and in recent years there has been a growing appreciation among some fishermen for the whitefish's sporting attributes, especially on flies during the winter.

Mountain whitefish are dull brown and average 1 to 2 lb/450 to 900 g, and seldom grow to more than 15 in/38 cm. They live in cold streams and rivers from the Yukon and British Columbia, down through the Rockies of Montana, Wyoming, and neighboring states to Nevada.

Long considered a sea-run strain of the rainbow trout, the steelhead is now classified as a Pacific salmon, along with the chinook, coho, and other members of the genus *Oncorhynchus.*

Cutthroat trout

Salmo clarki

DATA

Average weight: 1–2 lb/450–900 g.

North American record: 41 lb/18.6 kg; Pyramid Lake, Nevada, 1925.

Fishing tackle: Variety of spinning, fly gear; lures, flies, live bait.

Habitat: Streams, rivers, lakes.

Habits: Variety of distinct subspecies.

A bold slash of red or orange beneath the gill plates marks the cutthroat trout, endemic to the Rocky Mountains and one of the most variable trout in North America.

Dozens of subspecies have been described, not all of which have stood the test of later scientific scrutiny, but many are still recognized – populations that vary in form, reproductive behavior, and especially color from river system to river system. In northwest Wyoming, for example, the heavily spotted Snake River cutthroat is distinct from the more golden, lightly speckled Yellowstone cutt, which makes a spectacular spawning run up Yellowstone River toward Yellowstone Lake, leaping the LeHardy Rapids like salmon.

In most waters a 16-in/40-cm cutthroat is big, although a now-extinct subspecies in Pyramid Lake, Nevada, reached a much larger size, with one monster tipping the scale at 41 lb/18.6 kg. The cutthroat has been widely stocked, and thoughtless mingling of subspecies has in some waters blurred the unique, native stocks. A new emphasis on preserving the genetic integrity of each subspecies gives hope for the future, however.

Rainbow trout

Salmo gairdneri

DATA

Average weight: 1–2 lb/450–900 g.

Fishing tackle: Variety of spinning, fly gear.

Habitat: Streams, rivers, lakes.

Habits: Spectacular leaps when hooked.

Lewis and Clark dubbed this western species the "speckled mountain trout," a name that is, in its own way, as descriptive as "rainbow" – for most populations of this trout combine lovely shades of pink, red, and silver with a heavy peppering of fine black spots on the back, dorsal fin, and tail.

A fisherman can often guess the variety of trout on his line by the way it fights. The brook trout lacks staying power, the brown battles underwater, but the rainbow reaches for the sky again and again, leaping and cartwheeling when hooked, making it one of the world's most popular gamefish.

Stocked as far as Chile and New Zealand, the rainbow is native to the cold streams, rivers and lakes of the Pacific slope of the Continental Divide as far north as Alaska. It thrives under hatchery conditions, making it perfect for both aquaculture and stocking operations; most rainbows caught in the US are stocked for put-and-take fishing, and average under 1 ft/30 cm. In parts of its natural range, however, it can reach much greater sizes – Alaska, with its trophy rainbows, has become an angling mecca.

The steelhead, now classified as a Pacific salmon (*see* page 28), was for years thought to be a sea-run variety of the rainbow trout. A pale yellow color form of the rainbow, known as the palomino, is stocked as a novelty fish in some areas.

The Atlantic salmon has been called "the most perfect of fish;" while that may be an exaggeration, it is not much of one. This salmon has been the object of near-reverence by fly-fishermen for centuries – a sporting cult with its own traditions, even its own works of art, the gaudy salmon flies.

This venerated fish is actually a sea-run trout rather than a true salmon. In North America it is found from northern New England through the Canadian Maritimes; it is also found in Iceland and Europe. A landlocked form, known as sebago or ouananiche, occurs naturally in some lakes from Maine north, and may weigh 6 lb/ 2.7 kg pounds. Sea-going Atlantic salmon are much bigger, although because most salmon survive the spawning run to return in future years, there are usually many different sizes of Atlantic salmon in the river, from small grilse through 20- to 30-lb/9- to 14-kg adults. In parts of Scandinavia they grow even bigger, with monsters of nearly 80 lb/36 kg on record, and in recent years a few fish of 60 and 70 lb/27 and 32 kg have again come from Canadian rivers.

Atlantic salmon are beautifully streamlined, silvery-gray with a few black flecks on the sides and back; once in freshwater the male develops a kype, and the color dar-

Atlantic salmon

Salmo salar

DATA

Average weight: 15–20 lb/6.8–9 kg.

World record: 79 lb 2 oz/35.9 kg; Tana River, Norway, 1928.

Fishing tackle: Medium to heavy fly gear; beautifully dressed salmon flies.

Habitat: Rivers.

Habits: Sizzling runs and high leaps.

kens, but there is not the dramatic physical change that Pacific salmon undergo.

Pollution, overfishing, and dams eliminated Atlantic salmon runs on many New England rivers in the 18th and 19th centuries. Fisheries' managers have been working, with some notable successes, to restore these runs, but the Atlantic salmon in North America are still found mostly in the wilderness rivers of coastal Canada.

BELOW The Atlantic salmon – once described as "the most perfect of fish" – is in fact a sea-run trout rather than a true salmon. Its silvery-gray streamlined form is evident in this 27-lb/12-kg specimen.

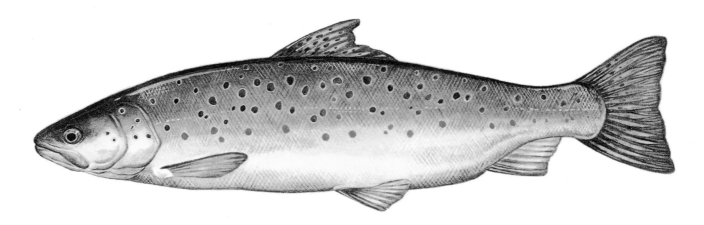

Brown trout

Salmo trutta

DATA

Average weight: 1–2 lb/450–900 g.

North American record: 34 lb 6 oz/ 15.6 kg; Bar Lake, Michigan, 1984.

Fishing tackle: Variety of fly and spinning gear.

Habitat: Streams, lakes, rivers.

Habits: Highly selective in heavily fished waters.

Pariah to savior – the brown trout's fortunes in North America have undergone a remarkable change in the years since this European import was released into the waters of the New World. At first, fishermen scorned it in favor of the brook trout, native to the cold streams of the East. But as development and land clearing left many streams tainted and warm, the brook trout faded away, to be replaced by the hardier brown trout, which is now the mainstay of fly-fishermen.

Identifying the various species of trout can be confusing, but not if you look at the spots. Brown trout can range in color from gold to silver, but they are usually spotted heavily on the back, with only indistinct spotting on the tail. Rainbow trout (which often lack a pink stripe) are heavily spotted on the tail and dorsal fin. Brook trout have wormlike vermiculations on the back, in addition to spots.

Brown trout are the most widely available of all the trout, found in almost every cold-water fishery in the United States, and parts of Canada. Millions are stocked each spring in put-and-take waters, but many survive to become canny holdovers; the selectivity of brown trout is legendary – and frustrating for the angler whose offering is repeatedly refused. Brown trout can reach enormous sizes, especially in large lakes and reservoirs, where 25-lb/11-kg brownies are not unheard of. Lake-run trout are usually silvery, while old stream fish are most often a rich yellow-brown.

Hybrid trout

Not satisfied with the array of trout species that nature has provided, fisheries' biologists have "created" some unusual hybrids, in the hope of combining the best characteristics of different species. While the results have been interesting, few have shown any great promise for sport fishermen, and are stocked only on an experimental basis.

The splake is a cross between the lake trout and brook (or speckled) trout; it grows faster than a lake trout, but reaches a larger size than a brookie. The tiger trout, a hybrid of a male brook trout and female brown, is named for its aggressive nature.

LEFT Brown trout can be exceptionally selective, especially when they have been fished for frequently, requiring a precise match between artificial fly and natural food.

LEFT Lake-run
brown trout, with
an abundance of
forage fish on which
to feed, grow to
spectacular sizes.

Arctic char

Salvelinus alpinus

Some of the brightest colors of the Arctic autumn are not the flaming red leaves of the dwarf blueberries, but the red sides of the spawning arctic char, which race the impending winter as they swim upstream from the ocean to breed.

Found across the sweep of the far north, from Labrador to Alaska, the arctic char is the least-known of North America's game-fish, sharing the land with caribou, wolves, and bears, but few people. Those who have caught char on sport tackle, however, find them full of fight – and find the orange flesh to be excellent, as well.

Sea-run arctic char average 3 to 5 lb/1.4 to 2.3 kg, with some exceeding 20 lb/9 kg.

DATA

Average weight: 3–5 lb/1.4–2.3 kg.

Fishing tackle: Medium spinning or fly gear; spoons, spinners, large flies.

Habitat: Rivers.

Habits: Anadromous.

Fresh from the ocean they resemble a large, silvery brook trout, but the males in particular quickly change color, developing large areas of red or orange on the belly and sides. A spawning char may be hard to tell from a large brookie; look for the char's absence of vermiculation on the back, dorsal fin, or tail, and the lack of blue rings around any red spots on the sides.

Landlocked holdovers from the last ice age, the blueback trout of Maine, and the Sunapee trout of northern New England are considered by some taxonomists as subspecies of the arctic char; the Quebec red trout is also sometimes lumped under the same heading.

Brook trout

Salvelinus fontinalis

In the crystalline waters of a mountain stream, a male brook trout passes through a shaft of sunlight – orange fins edged in black and white, a red belly that blends with purple flanks, a greenish back scrawled with lighter vermiculations, and spots of red haloed by blue.

The brook trout is the only native trout in the East – and it is not a true trout at all, but the most southern of the chars. It needs exceptionally cold, pure waters, and has been driven out of most lowland streams by human development, replaced by stocked trout. Ironically, streams that no longer support wild brook trout may receive stockings of hatchery brookies, fish with

DATA

Average weight: ½–1 lb/225–450 g.

North American record: 14 lb 8 oz/ 6.6 kg; Nipigon River, Ontario, 1916.

Fishing tackle: Light spinning or fly gear; spinners, small plugs, flies.

Habitat: Streams and rivers.

Habits: Needs cold, pure water.

little of the color and none of the spunk of their wild brethren.

Look for wild brook trout in headwater streams, where the shading forest keeps the water cold and free of sediment. Food is scarce in such fast-flowing creeks, and a brook trout may take years to reach 7 or 8 in/18 or 20 cm; a 12-in/30-cm specimen is a trophy, to be gently released after the fight. Brook trout originally were found from Labrador and Minnesota south through the Appalachians, but they have been widely stocked, especially in the Rockies. In parts of Canada, where fishing pressure is light, a trophy "squaretail" may weigh over 6 lb/ 2.7 kg.

Dolly Varden

Salvelinus malma

Rivers, streams, and lakes west of the Rockies are home to the Dolly Varden, named for a beautiful woman in a Dickens' novel, but derided as a killer of more desirable species.

There is no doubt that the Dolly Varden eats smaller fish, including the parr of salmon and trout – but so do rainbows, cutthroats, and other large gamefish, so there is no reason to single out the Dolly Varden for venom, as has long been the case. At one point Alaska even offered a bounty on this species of char, in a needless effort to "protect" its salmon fishery.

> **DATA**
>
> **Average weight:** 3–5 lb/1.4–2.3 kg.
>
> **Fishing tackle:** Medium spinning or fly gear.
>
> **Habitat:** Rivers, streams, lakes.
>
> **Habits:** Anadromous; some populations landlocked.

Dolly Vardens are mid-size chars, averaging up to 5 lb/2.3 kg. Color is highly variable, depending on what body of water the fish is taken from. However, the base color is usually greenish, blending to yellow-white on the belly, with light spots of yellow, orange, or red; the ventral fins may be reddish with white and black edging, like a brook trout's. Dolly Vardens in Alaska may be confused with arctic char, which tend to have larger spots.

The bull trout, once considered a form of the Dolly Varden, is now thought to be a distinct species.

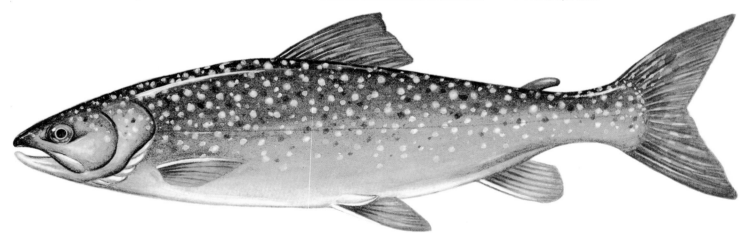

Lake trout

Salvelinus namaycush

One of the inland heavyweights, this species of char may grow to more than 70 lb/32 kg – a size that takes decades to achieve in the short growing seasons of the northern latitudes, where the biggest lake trout are now found.

Originally restricted to the deep, glacial lakes of the north, lake trout were especially common in the Great Lakes, supporting a vast sport and commercial fishery. But the accidental introduction of the sea lamprey devastated the lake trout, and the annual commercial catch dropped from 10 million

> **DATA**
>
> **Average weight:** 10–20 lb/4.5–9 kg.
>
> **North American record:** 65 lb/29.5 kg; Great Bear Lake, Northwest Territories, 1970.
>
> **Fishing tackle:** Heavy trolling gear; downriggers.
>
> **Habitat:** Lakes.
>
> **Habits:** Lives deep in large lakes.

lb/4.5 million kg to almost nothing in the 1950s. Aggressive lamprey control has improved the situation somewhat, but toxins washing into the lakes are apparently taking a toll on the trout, too, and numbers have not recovered to their former levels.

Lake trout are separated from other members of *Salvelinus* by their deeply forked tail. The body is whitish below, green above, with hundreds of pale white or yellow spots; in some lakes the base color is much paler. Lake trout are also known as gray trout, togue, or mackinaw.

Bounty of a
western river,
rainbow, brook,
and cutthroat trout
provide excellent
sport on a flyrod,
and are even better
in the pan.

Arctic grayling

Thymallus arcticus

The Arctic, or American, grayling's unusual genus name comes from the odd smell of its flesh, which reminds many people of freshly picked thyme. The grayling's greatest claim to fame, though, is its spectacular dorsal fin, which rises like a sail above the back.

The grayling is most common from northwestern Canada to Alaska, but relict populations, hinting of a time when the climate was cooler, also exist in Montana and Utah. Early in the 20th century another variety

DATA

Average weight: ½–2 lb/225–900 g.

Fishing tackle: Light spinning or fly gear; tiny spinners, plugs, small flies.

Habitat: Rivers, streams, lakes.

Habits: Often found in even-size schools.

was criminally driven to extinction in Michigan through overfishing and habitat destruction.

A grayling is not a fish that is easily mistaken for any other. Most are silvery to iridescent purple, with dark flecks on the forward half of the body and light spots on the sail. Alaskan grayling average 1 lb/450 g, and rarely exceed 4 lb/1.8 kg. Montana grayling are smaller, with a smaller dorsal sail, and in all varieties the male's fin is bigger than the female's.

FAMILY OSMERIDAE

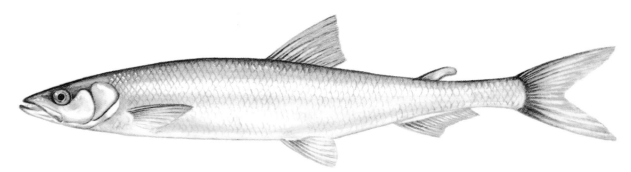

Rainbow smelt

Osmerus mordax

Slim and tasty, the rainbow smelt is a favorite for both its sport and table value. Native to the northern reaches of both coasts and New England, and introduced to the Great Lakes, it is a schooling fish, forming tremendous shoals. Each individual is elongated and vaguely trout-like in shape, silvery, with an underslung jaw and lots of sharp teeth. An adipose fin separates it from the similar, but unrelated, silversides. The maximum size is about 13 in/33 cm, and most are only half that.

DATA

Average length: 6–10 in/15–25 cm.

Fishing tackle: Nets; ice fishing gear with smelt skin as bait.

Habitat: Rivers, lakes.

Habits: Anadromous; some landlocked populations.

Rainbow smelt are anadromous, although many landlocked populations exist. An early spring spawning run is made not long after ice-out, and before overfishing depleted the stocks, most smelt rivers held incredible numbers of these small fish. During the spawning run smelt are usually netted, but ice-fishing with rod and line is popular on many lakes; the best bait is often a strip of skin from another smelt, although a substitute of perch skin, or some other fish, can suffice.

FAMILY ESOCIDAE

The smallest member of the genus E*sox*, the redfin pickerel lacks the size of the muskellunge or northern pike, but retains their audacity and appetite.

All members of the genus are slim, highly predatory fish, with dorsal fins set far down the back and wide, almost duckbill, mouths. The redfin pickerel has vertical barring on the sides; the reddish fins are not a definitive field mark, since almost any member of the pike family may show the color. The

Redfin pickerel

Esox americanus

DATA

Average weight: ½ lb/225 g.

Fishing tackle: Poor sport fish; caught on light tackle.

Habitat: Lakes, ponds, rivers.

Habits: Ambush hunter like larger relatives.

surest method of separating the redfin from the chain pickerel is to count the branchiostegal rays: a redfin has 13 or fewer, and a chain has 14 or more.

Redfin pickerel are seldom more than 1 ft/30 cm long, average ½ lb/225 g in weight, and are of little sport value. They are strictly eastern; a subspecies, the grass pickerel (E. *a. vermiculatus*), is found in the western drainage of the Appalachians, and is virtually identical.

Anything that moves, and can barely squeeze down its tooth-lined maw, counts as food for the northern pike, a rapacious feeder that is also a superior gamefish.

Northern pike get large, regularly up to 20 lb/9 kg, sometimes in excess of 40 lb/ 18 kg. There is little variation in color – green with a white belly, liberally covered with oblong, yellowish spots; the fins may have a distinct reddish cast. Pike occur naturally within the range of ancient glaciation, from Labrador to Alaska and south to New England and British Columbia, but have

Northern pike

Esox lucius

DATA

Average weight: 8–15 lb/3.6–6.8 kg.

World record: 55 lb 1 oz/25 kg; West Germany, 1986.

Fishing tackle: Casting, spinning or fly gear; variety of large lures, live bait.

Habitat: Lakes.

Habits: Often in shallow, stump- or weed-choked coves.

been stocked in artificial lakes far beyond those boundaries.

Because pike are such indiscriminate feeders, a wide variety of bait and lures will take them, although spoons, spinners, plugs and live minnows are traditional favorites. In lakes where walleyes or smallmouth bass are the prime quarry, northerns have long been scorned as worthless "snakes," but more and more anglers are realizing the sporting value of these bruising fighters.

The muskellunge is the toughest North American freshwater fish to catch. Populations are never high, even in good habitat, and anglers must resign themselves to hundreds of hours of casting, on average, for every trophy of this sort brought to boat.

Muskellunge

Esox masquinongy

DATA

Average weight: 15–20 lb/6.8–9 kg.

North American record: 69 lb 15 oz/ 31.7 kg; St Lawrence River, 1957.

Fishing tackle: Casting or spinning gear; large plugs, spinners, spoons.

Habitat: Lakes, rivers.

Habits: Unpredictable, difficult to catch.

More than a good boat and lots of lures, a muskellunge fisherman needs patience, for the muskie is the hardest of all freshwater gamefish to bring to the strike. The ratio runs to hundreds of hours fishing for every trophy boated.

The muskie is, with the lake trout, white sturgeon, and chinook salmon, among the biggest of freshwater fish. It is certainly the most predaceous, feeding heavily on other fish, as well as small mammals, birds, reptiles, amphibians, and anything else that makes the mistake of coming too close. The record fish, at nearly 70 lb/32 kg, was un-usual, but many muskies in the 35- to 45-lb/ 16- to 20-kg range have been caught.

A mature muskellunge can only be confused with a northern pike, but is far less colorful than its smaller relative, with a green-gray or brownish background tone, and often indistinct dark spotting or vertical bars. The large pores on the underside of the jaw provide a firm clue – six or more per side in the muskie, and five or less on a northern. The muskellunge occurs in lakes and rivers from the Great Lakes region to parts of New England and south (via introductions) through the Ohio Valley.

Chain pickerel

Esox niger

DATA

Average weight: 1–2 lb/450–900 g.

North American record: 9 lb 6 oz/4.3 kg; Homerville, Georgia, 1961.

Fishing tackle: Light gear; spinners, plugs, small spoons, flies, live bait.

Habitat: Lakes, streams.

Habits: Drifts quietly near cover, waiting for food.

Seemingly a smaller version of the northern pike, the chain pickerel has dark, chain-like markings on its sides, and inhabits a much more southerly range than its bigger cousin, from Florida and the Gulf up the coastal plain to New England, and in the lower Mississippi Valley.

Found both in sluggish streams and still water, the pickerel hunts by ambush, as do all the pikes, lunging at the last moment with its jaws gaping. Although the pickerel usually grows to no more than 18 in/46 cm, it is a spirited fighter, especially on light tackle. While most are taken accidently by bass fishermen, some are purposely sought out by those who appreciate their spunk.

In waters where pickerel and northern pike both occur, check the opercle for an identification – the pickerel's is completely scaled, while the pike's is scaled only on the upper half.

FAMILY CYPRINIDAE

Common carp

Cyprinus carpio

DATA

Average weight: 5–20 lb/2.3–9 kg.

North American record: 57 lb 13 oz/ 26.2 kg; Tidal Basic, Washington, DC, 1983.

Fishing tackle: Medium to heavy gear; worms, corn, scented doughballs.

Habitat: Lakes, rivers.

Habits: Bottom-feeder; may form large schools.

Some things are better left undone, and North America's fisheries would be in much better shape had the introduction of the common carp been one of them.

Sadly, this heaviest of the minnow family (native to Asia) was successfully introduced into the United States from Germany in the 1870s, and has spread far and wide since then. Its proliferation was often engineered with human assistance – despite the fact that the carp seriously degrades its habitat by uprooting aquatic vegetation and roiling the water, as well as overpopulating to the detriment of native species.

Carp have a high, humped back, brassy color, and two small barbels beside the downturned mouth. They can grow to more than 30 in/76 cm and 60 lb/27 kg, and even though they are considered a trash fish, large carp fight like snagged submarines. Tolerant of warm water and found almost everywhere from southern Canada to the Mexican border, carp provide sport fishing where virtually nothing else can.

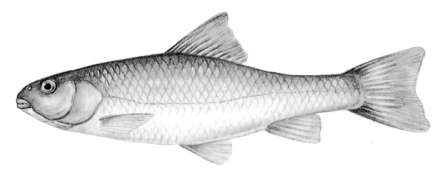

Cutlips minnow

Exoglossum maxillingua

DATA

Average length: 2–6 in/5–15 cm.

Habitat: Streams, rivers.

Habits: Often found in rocky riffles.

One of the common minnows of eastern streams, the cutlips is also one of the easiest in this confusing family to identify. Viewed in the hand from below, the lower lip is divided into three lobes, the middle protruding beyond the other two like a tongue being stuck out. The cutlips is olive-brown above and lighter below, without a distinct dark line. The maximum size is about 6 in/15 cm.

Cutlips minnows are found in streams and cool rivers from Virginia to the St Lawrence valley. A similar species, the tonguetied minnow (E. *laurae*) is found in the southern Appalachians; this minnow can be distinguished by the less pronounced central lip lobe, and there may be small barbels at the corners of the mouth.

Hornyhead chub

Nocomis biguttatus

DATA

Average length: 4–8 in/10–20 cm.

Habitat: Streams, rivers.

Habits: Males build and defend nest on stream bottom.

In the spring breeding season, the males of this medium-sized minnow develop horny tubercles on the head, complimenting the red spot behind each eye. A dark band extends from the snout down the length of the body, ending in a distinct caudal spot. The dorsal half of the chub is olive, fading to yellowish on the sides, and there are tiny barbels at the corners of the mouth.

Hornyhead chubs have a wide range, and are found in clear, slow-moving streams and rivers from Wyoming to New York, and south to the southern Plains states; they appear highly sensitive to sediment pollution. An important forage species for gamefish, hornyhead chubs are often used for bait, and reach a maximum length of 8 to 10 in/20 to 25 cm.

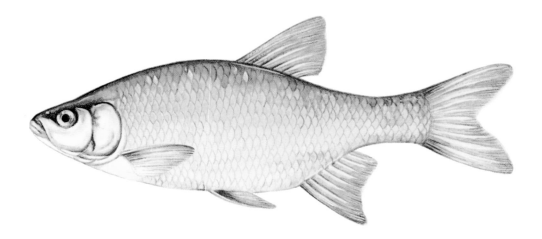

Golden shiner

Notemigonus crysoleucas

DATA

Average length: 4–8 in/10–20 cm.

Habitat: Lakes, ponds, rivers.

Habits: Often found near aquatic weed beds.

From the peat-stained ponds of the New England mountains to placid swamps in Florida, schools of golden shiners are a common sight.

Deeper-bodied than most minnows, golden shiners gleam like polished brass, although in some bodies of water they are pale silver instead. Growing up to 1 ft/ 30 cm long, shiners are important food fish for pike, bass, pickerel, herons, osprey, and river otters; they in turn feed on tiny aquatic insects and plants. They are found from southern Canada to the Gulf, and as far west as Texas and Saskatchewan.

Golden shiners do well in captivity, are hardy in transit and on the hook, making them among the most popular of baitfish. In some areas they are considered a minor sportfish in their own right, although most caught on light tackle are intended for use as live bait for trophy muskies, pike, or largemouth bass.

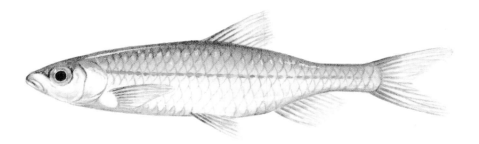

Emerald shiner

Notropis atherinoides

One of the slimmest of the common varieties of shiners, the emerald shiner schools in tremendous numbers in large rivers, reservoirs, and lakes, showing a preference for clear, silt-free water.

The emerald shiner is usually no more than 3 in/7.5 cm long, with an indistinct lateral band and a wash of pale, iridescent green along the dorsal surface, especially

DATA

Average length: 1–3 in/2.5–7.5 cm.

Habitat: Lakes, rivers.

Habits: Forms large schools at mid-water depths.

toward the tail. The dorsal fin begins slightly behind the leading edge of the pelvic fins, and all the fins are unmarked.

Emerald shiners are found from the St Lawrence River valley to the Northwest Territories and south through virtually all of the Mississippi drainage. Wherever it is found, it is an important forage species for gamefish.

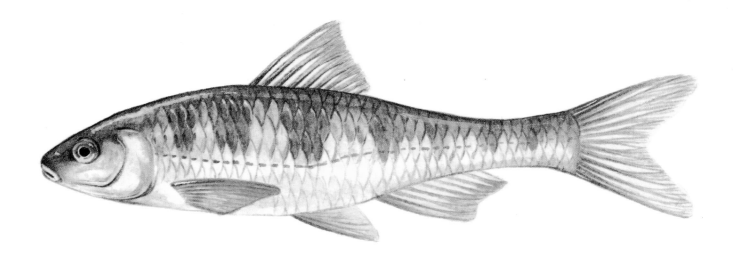

Common shiner

Notropis cornutus

Another extremely important baitfish, the common shiner is abundant in a band across the northern United States and southern Canada, as far west as Colorado and Saskatchewan.

Blunt-headed and growing to a length of as much as 10 in/25 cm, the common shiner is covered with large, silvery-blue scales, and often shows a number of irregular dark blotches on the sides, which resemble

DATA

Average length: 4–8 in/10–20 cm.

Habitat: Streams, rivers.

Habits: Intolerant of warm water.

missing scales. The fins – especially the pelvic fins – are edged with red, and the colors become more pronounced in the spring spawning season, when the male's body color also changes, taking on a deep bluish-purple tone.

Common shiners are most often found in cool streams and rivers, and do not have the tolerance for warm water exhibited by chubs, which they somewhat resemble.

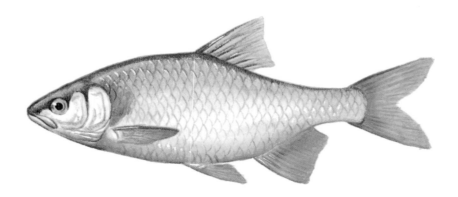

Red shiner

Notropis lutrensis

DATA

Average length: 1–3 in/2.5–7.5 cm.

Habitat: Streams, rivers.

Habits: Highly tolerant of silty water.

Despite its name, the red shiner is, like most of its genus, a silvery fish overall, but the spawning male has a bright orange belly and crimson ventral fins and tail, making it attractive enough at one time to warrant attention as an aquarium fish.

This species has a deeply compressed body similar to a golden shiner, with dark blue-gray pigmentation on the dorsal surface and silver sides; females lack the male's bright coloration, and may appear greenish. At full growth, a red shiner is usually less than 3 in/7.5 cm long.

Red shiners are native to the continent's midsection, in streams and small rivers cutting through the Plains from the Dakotas to south Texas, and from the western Mississippi drainage to Wyoming. They have been introduced over much of the rest of the United States and parts of Canada.

Northern redbelly dace

Phoxinus eos

DATA

Average length: 1–2 in/2.5–5 cm.

Habitat: Streams.

Habits: Diet primarily algae growing in mud.

This is one of the prettiest minnows in North America, especially when the males take on their most vibrant colors for the breeding season. The redbelly has a three-part lateral stripe – two thin black bands separated by a pale streak – with bright red on the lower sides, throat, and chin, as well as a red spot at the base of the dorsal fin; the ventral fins become lemon-yellow. The effect is almost tropical, even though this small minnow (maximum size 3 in/7.5 cm) inhabits only ice-cold mountain streams.

Northern redbelly daces are found from Nova Scotia to British Columbia and south to the Rockies and northern Appalachians; the closely related southern redbelly is native to the Midwest, and the mountain redbelly dace to parts of the James River drainage. Wherever they are found, these daces are considered superb baitfish among trout fishermen, who believe that the brilliant colors of the males add to the bait's attractiveness. They are not hardy, needing cold, well-oxygenated water to survive.

Bluntnose minnow

Pimephales notatus

The bluntnose minnow is common in silty, slow-moving creeks, small lakes, and rivers ranging from southern New England to the northern Plains, and south to Oklahoma and Louisiana.

It is easily distinguished from the black-nose dace by its rounder head and somewhat bigger mouth, which is underslung but not as sharply downturned as in the dace.

DATA

Average length: 2–3 in/5–7.5 cm.

Habitat: Streams, rivers, lakes.

Habits: Spawning lasts from early spring to fall; male guards eggs and fry.

The bluntnose is olivish above and pale below, with a dark lateral stripe and a black spot at the base of the tail, and reaches a maximum length of about 4 in/10 cm.

The bluntnose minnow may be confused with the similar cutlips minnow, which is easily distinguished by the odd shape of its tri-lobed lower lip and lack of a clearly defined lateral stripe.

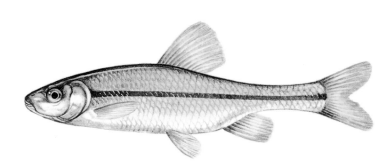

Fathead minnow

Pimephales promelas

The fathead minnow's small size belies its abundance and extremely wide range – native to all but the Arctic, far West and extreme South, and introduced in many locations from the Rockies to the Pacific.

An adult fathead rarely exceeds 2½ in/ 6 cm, and most individuals are half that size, making them an important food for the young of most game species that share its preference for cool, clear streams.

DATA

Average length: 1 in/2.5 cm.

Habitat: Streams.

Habits: Male develops spawning colors.

The fathead minnow is olive, often with a hint of iridescence, and an incomplete lateral stripe; the best field mark is the dark band across the middle of the dorsal fin, which unfortunately is only present in adults. In the spawning season males develop a heavy, tubercled pad on the nape of the neck, and have two diffuse, vertical gold bands on the body – one behind the head, the other under the dorsal fin.

Squawfish belong to the Family Cyprinidae, but they are hardly "minnows" in the usual sense of the word. The northern squawfish, the most widespread of the group, may be more than 2 ft/60 cm long, and other species get even bigger.

Northern squawfish are long, slim fish, somewhat pike-like in shape, greenish-brown above and pale on the ventral surface; the mouth is quite large for a minnow. They are found in coastal streams of Washington and Oregon, as well as the

Northern squawfish

Ptychocheilus oregonensis

DATA

Average weight: 4–6 lb/1.8–2.7 kg.

Fishing tackle: Light or medium gear; small lures or live bait.

Habitat: Streams, rivers.

Habits: Agile fish-eater.

Columbia River drainage as far south as northern Nevada.

The Colorado squawfish, growing to a length of 5 ft/1.5 m and weights of more than 80 lb/36 kg, is the largest of all North American minnows. Restricted to the lower Colorado River, it has suffered from human development, and is a federally protected endangered species.

The blacknose dace is one of the most familiar stream minnows within its range, found in cool, moving waters from Nova Scotia to the Dakotas, and south through the southern Appalachians.

Like most minnows it has a slim, stream-lined shape (vaguely humpbacked in this case), with a slightly downturned snout and a small mouth. The back is brown, some-times with gold highlights, and the belly is

Blacknose dace

Rhinichthys atratulus

DATA

Average length: 2–4 in/5–10 cm.

Habitat: Streams, rivers.

Habits: Prefers faster water with rocky bottom.

white; they are separated by a dark line that runs the length of the body. A dark stripe alone does not make a minnow a blacknose dace – the identifying charac-teristics are the heaviness of the line, the size of the mouth, and the presence of a tiny barbel at each corner of the mouth.

Blacknose daces are a favorite forage species for trout and smallmouth bass, and so are often used by fishermen as bait.

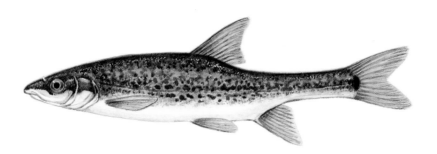

The most widespread of the daces, the longnose dace is found from New England through the Appalachians, across the Great Lakes and southern Canada to the Yukon, the Pacific Northwest and south through the Rockies to the Mexican border; a disjunct population is also found in the eastern Arctic. Wherever it occurs, it prefers riffles in clear, cold streams, as its specific name, *cataractae*, would indicate. Its major

Longnose dace

Rhinichthys cataractae

DATA

Average length: 2–4 in/5–10 cm.

Habitat: Streams.

Habits: Eats primarily blackfly larvae.

food appears to be blackfly larvae, which also require exceptionally clean water.

The longnose dace is similar to the blacknose, but is more heavily mottled along the lateral line; the snout is also noticeably longer, and overhangs the small mouth like a proboscis. As with all members of the genus *Rhinichthys*, there are barbels at the corners of the mouth. The maximum length is about 4 or 5 in/10 or 13 cm.

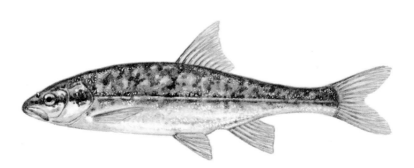

The western counterpart to the blacknose dace, the speckled dace is found on the western drainage of the Rockies, from Washington to Arizona.

In shape it is similar to the longnose and blacknose daces, but the speckled lacks a distinct lateral stripe, and is not as heavily mottled as the longnose. While the mouth is somewhat underslung, it lacks the pro-

Speckled dace

Rhinichthys osculus

DATA

Average length: 2–4 in/5–10 cm.
Habitat: Streams, rivers, lakes.
Habits: Some subspecies tolerant of very warm water.

nounced snout of the longnose dace. Maximum size is about 4 in/10 cm.

As might be expected for a fish found over such a wide area, the speckled dace has a number of subspecies, including one capable of surviving water temperatures of more than 80 degrees Fahrenheit/26 degrees Celsius – levels that would be lethal to most other daces.

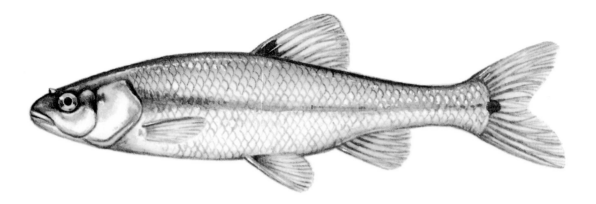

Detested by fishermen for their utter abandon when feeding (because they usually hit the lure before a trout has a chance), creek chubs are one of the bigger minnows within their range, growing to about 1 ft/30 cm.

A creek chub has a blunt, round head and silvery color that dulls to brown in the back. A dark lateral stripe is usually present,

Creek chub

Semotilus atromaculatus

DATA

Average length: 6–12 in/15–30 cm.

Habitat: Streams, rivers.

Habits: Often feeds on surface, like a rising trout.

as is a dark spot at the base of the dorsal fin, which is the best field mark. Inhabiting streams and rivers, it is found from eastern Canada to the Rockies, ranging southwards to the Gulf.

In spring, males develop hard tubercles on the top of the head, and in some areas the species is known as the horned chub.

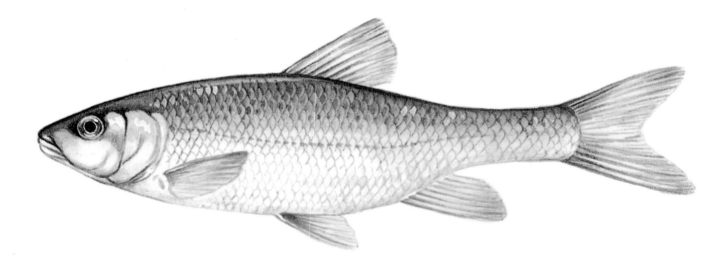

A larger version of the creek chub, the fallfish may attain lengths of 17 in/43 cm, and is such a hard fighter some anglers accord it gamefish status, although in most waters it is considered a trash fish.

Brassier in color than the creek chub, the fallfish lacks the chub's dorsal spot, and is found in colder, fast-moving waters. Like the chub, the spawning males develop tubercles on the head, and their sides take on a rosy flush. It has a rather restricted range,

Fallfish

Semotilus corporalis

DATA

Average length: 10–15 in/25–38 cm.

Habitat: Streams, rivers.

Habits: Takes flies and lures readily.

from the James Bay and St Lawrence River drainages south between the Appalachians and coast to Virginia.

FAMILY CATOSTOMIDAE

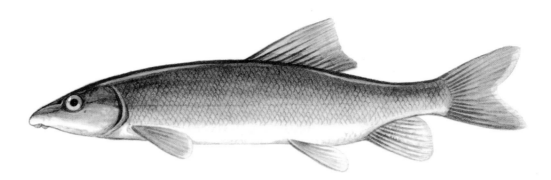

Longnose sucker

Catostomus catostomus

A deepwater species except during the spawning season, the longnose sucker inhabits large, cold lakes across Canada and the northern tier of North American states, as far south as the Columbia drainage and West Virginia.

Longnose suckers reach a length of 18 or 20 in/46 or 51 cm, and may weigh 5 or 6 lb/2.3 or 2.7 kg. They are dark olive-brown on the back and white below, with a hint of a lateral stripe. The best field mark, however, is the large, pointed, protruding snout, which extends well beyond the mouth. The scales are smaller than in other suckers, and the lower lip is almost completely divided into two sections.

The longnose sucker may be found at depths as great as 600 ft/183 m, and is of little sport value in lakes. During the spring it ascends tributary creeks to spawn and may be taken on light tackle, providing a spirited fight.

DATA

Average weight: 2–3 lb/900–1400 g.

Fishing tackle: Light gear; small lures or bait.

Habitat: Lakes.

Habits: Makes spawning runs up tributary streams.

White sucker

Catostomus commersoni

White suckers are found over most of North America, absent only from the South, extreme Arctic and far West. They are also the only member of the family to have significant sport value, although they are not considered a true gamefish.

Like all suckers, the white has a downturned, fleshy mouth used to grub for food among the bottom sediments. Its color varies somewhat from region to region, but most have an olivish dorsal surface fading to white underneath, with a hint of gold on the sides; some populations are much brassier. The scales are large and coarse. Maximum size is about 2 ft/60 cm, and maximum weight is 8 lb/3.6 kg.

White suckers are found in lakes, rivers, and large streams, and during the early spring spawning run are often found in tremendous numbers in quite small rivulets. Although not a very good food fish because of its bony flesh, the sucker is avidly sought by sport anglers and spear-fishermen in some areas.

DATA

Average weight: 1–3 lb/400–1400 g.

Fishing tackle: Light spinning gear; corn, worms, doughballs.

Habitat: Lakes, rivers, streams.

Habits: Makes spawning runs up tributary streams.

Northern hog sucker

Hypentilium nigricans

DATA

Average weight: 1–2 lb/450–900 g.

Habitat: Streams, rivers.

Habits: Feed by rolling rocks over.

In streams and rivers, much of the insect life is hidden beneath rocks, safe from most predators – but not from the northern hog sucker. This fish uses its large, bony head and long snout to pry the rocks over, then vacuums off the larvae of caddisflies, mayflies, and other insects.

Hog suckers are instantly recognizable by their big, boxy heads, which have a dished-out depression between the eyes, and by the four or five dark bands that drape over the back and sides. They reach a length of about 2 ft/60 cm and a maximum weight of several pounds/kilograms, although most are much smaller, especially in creeks.

Northern hog suckers (also known as hog mollies) are found from southern New England to Minnesota, and south to Alabama.

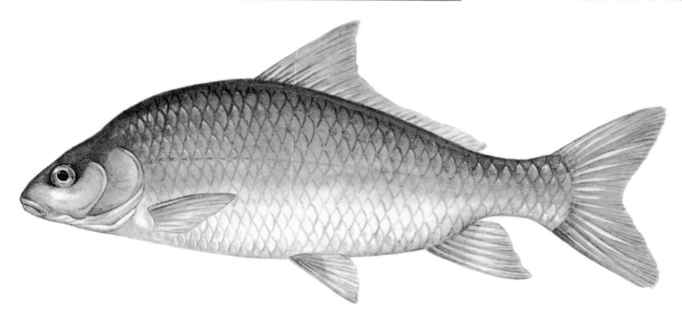

Smallmouth buffalo

Ictiobus bubalus

DATA

Average weight: 2–5 lb/900 g–2.3 kg.

Fishing tackle: Usually caught by accident on light tackle.

Habitat: Lakes, rivers.

Habits: Feeds largely on tiny bottom organisms.

This species has been confused with a carp more than once, since it has the same large-scaled, humpbacked appearance – which also explains its odd name, usually corrupted to "buffalofish." It is also known by the names roachback and thicklipped buffalo.

Buffalo are the largest of the suckers, and although the smallmouth does not reach the tremendous weights credited to the bigmouth buffalo, it may still exceed 40 lb/18 kg. The color ranges from olive to brassy, with gold tones especially evident on the sides. The dorsal fin extends most of the way to the tail, and the first rays are elongated; however, they are neither tapered nor as long as in the related quillback. Unlike other suckers, the mouths of the buffalos are not underslung – terminal rather than inferior, in the words of ichthyologists.

Smallmouth buffalo are common in lakes and slow rivers of the entire Mississippi drainage and southern Plains, including the Rio Grande system.

Bigmouth buffalo

Ictiobus cyprinellus

> ### DATA
>
> **Average weight:** 5–10 lb/2.3–4.5 kg.
>
> **Fishing tackle:** Usually caught accidentally.
>
> **Habitat:** Rivers, lakes.
>
> **Habits:** Feeds primarily on plankton.

Largest of the suckers, this prairie leviathan has been recorded weighing more than 80 lb/36 kg, although 10-lb/14.5-kg specimens are much more common.

The bigmouth buffalo (also commonly known as the largemouth, or lake, buffalo) closely resembles the smallmouth. For identification, note the relative placement of the mouth and the eye; in the bigmouth the upper lip begins at about the same level as the lower edge of the eye, while in the smallmouth the mouth is tiny, and is far down on the head.

Bigmouth buffalo apparently feed on plankton, small fish, and bottom matter, and are – like the smallmouth buffalo – rarely caught by sport fishermen. The species is found in a similar range to the smallmouth and is most common in the northern Plains and Mississippi system.

Shorthead redhorse

Moxostoma macrolepidotum

> ### DATA
>
> **Average weight:** 2–5 lb/900 g–2.3 kg.
>
> **Fishing tackle:** Light to medium gear; live bait.
>
> **Habitat:** Streams, rivers, lakes.
>
> **Habits:** Makes spring spawning runs up small creeks.

Commonly known as the northern redhorse, the shorthead redhorse is a colorful sucker, combining silver or gold on the body with bright red fins and tail. The dorsal fin is high and pointed, and usually paler than the other fins.

The shorthead is common in swift, cool streams, rivers, and lakes across the northern United States as far west as the Rockies, and north through much of Canada. It grows to more than 2 ft/60 cm, and weights of 10 lb/4.5 kg or more. The head is shorter than in most suckers, and the mouth, while underslung, is not as pronounced a "sucker" as in others of the family.

Redhorses are an important sport fish in some waters, and are more highly regarded as table fare than other suckers. They are the subject of localized commercial fisheries.

FAMILY ICTALURIDAE

White catfish

Ictalurus catus

> **DATA**
>
> **Average weight:** ½–1 lb/225–450 g.
>
> **Fishing tackle:** Light gear; live bait or stinkbaits.
>
> **Habitat:** Streams, rivers.
>
> **Habits:** Tolerant of brackish water.

The "Potomac catfish," as it is known in the Chesapeake region, is among the smaller members of the true catfish clan, usually reaching a size of only 1 lb/450 g.

The white catfish is pale blue-gray above and silver underneath, with a forked, somewhat rounded tail and a complete absence of spots (some specimens may, however, show a varying degree of mottling). It is found in slow-moving streams and rivers, and can tolerate brackish water. Its natural range is from the Chesapeake south to the Gulf, but it has been stocked also as far north as New England and west as far as the Pacific coast.

White catfish are commonly taken by sport anglers, although their small size relegates them to minor status as a gamefish.

Blue catfish

Ictalurus furcatus

> **DATA**
>
> **Average weight:** 10–15 lb/4.5–6.8 kg.
>
> **Fishing tackle:** Heavy casting gear; live, cut, or stinkbaits.
>
> **Habitat:** Rivers.
>
> **Habits:** Migratory; needs clear water.

The Goliath of its family, the blue catfish may weigh nearly 100 lb/45 kg, and 19th-century records hint at even greater sizes, in excess of 150 lb/68 kg. The average catch, however, weighs between 10 and 15 lb/4.5 and 6.8 kg.

Sadly, the blue catfish has suffered a serious decline in some parts of its range, where dams have eliminated much of its preferred habitat – clear, flowing water over a mud-free bottom – and made it impossible for these migratory fish to reach their spawning grounds. It occurred naturally from the northern Mississippi and Ohio rivers to the Gulf, but is now much more common in the southern half of its territory. It has been stocked elsewhere.

Blue catfish are blue-gray above and white below, very similar to the white catfish. The key difference is the number of rays in the anal fin – 30 or more for the blue, and between 19 and 23 for the white.

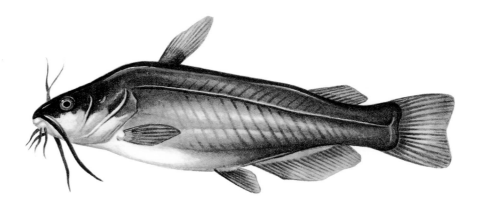

The four common species of bullheads are confusingly similar, and most anglers simply lump them together as "catties," since they look, feed, and act so much alike.

The black bullhead is one of the smaller members of this subgroup of catfish, with an average size of 1 lb/450 g and a maximum of about 7 or 8 lb/3.2 or 3.6 kg. It is found in ponds and lakes of the continental heartland, from New York to the Dakotas and south to Texas, and has been stocked almost everywhere else south of Canada.

Black bullhead

Ictalurus melas

DATA

Average weight: ½–1 lb/225–450 g.

Fishing tackle: Light gear; variety of baits.

Habitat: Lakes, ponds.

Habits: Feeds most actively at night.

Black bullheads may be black, dark brown, or mottled, but can be identified by the absence of serrations on the pectoral fin spines. Grip the spine lightly at its base and run your thumb along it to the tip; on a black bullhead, you will feel no barbs.

Occurring over much the same range as the black bullhead, the yellow bullhead is liable to be found in almost any pond or lake from the Dakotas to the Atlantic, and as far south as the Gulf coast.

Color is extremely variable, ranging from brown to almost black; only the belly is yellowish, and by no means is this coloration exhibited by every yellow bullhead. Look instead at the chin barbels, which in this species are light, rather than black or brown as in the other bullheads. Maximum size is 12–18 in/30–46 cm.

Yellow bullhead

Ictalurus natalis

DATA

Average weight: ½–1 lb/225–450 g.

Fishing tackle: Light gear; variety of baits.

Habitat: Lakes, ponds.

Habits: Hunts largely by scent.

A catfish's facial barbels are often mistakenly considered venomous, when in fact they are only harmless sensory organs. The spines at the leading edge of the dorsal and pectoral fins, however, can inflict a puncture wound if the fish is handled carelessly, and a mild irritant secreted by glands below the spines can make the experience a sore one.

Brown bullhead

Ictalurus nebulosus

DATA

Average weight: ½ lb/225 g.

Fishing tackle: Light gear; variety of baits.

Habitat: Lakes, ponds, rivers.

Habits: Tadpole-sized young may form dense, ball-like schools near shore.

Like all bullheads, the brown bullhead is a bottom feeder, scavenging for morsels of food it detects with its sensitive barbels. A gob of worms, a scented doughball, or a live crayfish will quickly attract it, especially at night – a reason why the best fishing for these common stillwater catfish is after the sun goes down.

Bullheads are not spectacular fighters, tugging doggedly but affording no thrills. They are good in the pan, however, and the growing market for their sweet flesh has led to mass aquaculture on catfish "farms" in the South, along with channel catfish. Domesticated or wild, the brown bullhead is one of the most popular.

This species is very similar to the other bullheads, but has strongly serrated pectoral spines, longer upper barbels, and is usually mottled with brown. It is native to the eastern two-thirds of North America, and has been stocked through most of the West. In size and habits it is much like the other bullheads, although the brown bullhead is more tolerant of moving water than the yellow or black.

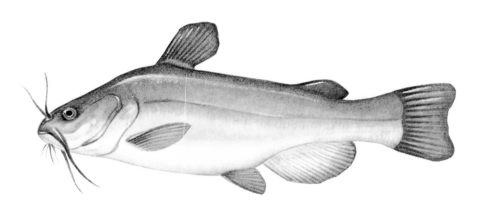

Snail bullhead

Ictalurus brunneus

DATA

Average weight: ¼–½ lb/110–225 g.
Habitat: Rivers, streams.
Habits: Prefers fast-moving water.

Small and of little significance as a sport fish, the snail, or green, bullhead is found in rivers in the southern coastal plain, from North Carolina to Florida. It resembles the brown bullhead but has fewer anal fin rays (17–20, rather than 20–30). The snail bullhead also lacks mottling, but the greenish coloration for which it was once named is not always apparent, and many specimens are solid brown.

The snail bullhead is small, usually under 1 ft/30 cm in length and ½ lb/225 g in weight.

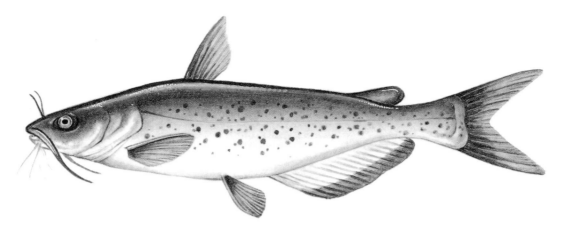

Channel catfish

Ictalurus punctatus

The most popular game species among the catfish, the channel cat is a hard-fighting inhabitant of rivers, large streams, and lakes, growing to a tackle-testing weight of more than 40 lb/18 kg.

The channel catfish is more streamlined than most of its relatives, an indication of its more active lifestyle away from the bottom; it is not unusual, in fact, to catch this species on mid-water or even surface lures. The tail is deeply forked, and the body color ranges from blue-gray above to white below, with scattered dark spots.

DATA

Average weight: 3–5 lb/1.4–2.3 kg.

Fishing tackle: Light to medium gear; jigs, plugs, spinners, live bait, trotlines.

Habitat: Rivers, lakes.

Habits: Active hunter, especially at night.

Channel cats occur naturally from the Great Lakes to Saskatchewan and south to Mexico, but because they are such a popular sport fish, they have been stocked in almost every suitable impoundment outside their range, as well. In some areas, night fishing for trophy channel catfish, using minnows as bait, is a top sport.

Stonecat

Noturus flavus

A stonecat is not much to look at – just a small, blandly colored catfish – but it packs a nasty punch in its pectoral spines, which are connected to rather potent venom glands. That is not to say that the stonecat or the closely related madtoms are dangerous, just that the wounds inflicted by their serrated pectoral spines sting and burn quite a bit more than similar wounds from other catfish.

Stonecats are found from the eastern Great Lakes to the Rockies, and south to

DATA

Average length: 4–8 in/10–20 cm.

Habitat: Rivers, streams.

Habits: Often hide under rocks.

Texas, inhabiting fast water and riffles where they can hide under loose rocks. An exceptional specimen will be 10 to 12 in/25–30 cm long, while most are no more than 6 in/15 cm. The color is solid, usually a dull yellow-brown or dingy gray. Stonecats are an important forage fish, especially for smallmouth bass, and are popular baitfish – as long as you are very careful where you put your fingers.

The madtoms are a large and confusing group of small catfish, with 25 species found generally in the South and Midwest. The tadpole madtom is more widespread than most of its relatives, found in slow streams and ponds from Saskatchewan to New York and south to the Gulf; it is also found in waters of the Atlantic coastal plain.

Unlike most madtoms, the tadpole madtom does not have a severely compressed

Tadpole madtom

Noturus gyrinus

DATA

Average length: 2–4 in/5–10 cm.

Habitat: Ponds, streams.

Habits: Hides much of the day among bottom debris.

head for living under rocks, but is built – as it name suggests – like a tadpole, with a bluntly rounded head and chunky body. It is usually yellowish-gray or brown, and rarely exceeds 4 in/10 cm. Like the other madtoms it has functional venom glands at the base of the pectoral spines, but despite them the tadpole madtom is a popular food fish for game species, and is often used as a baitfish by anglers.

The flathead catfish does, indeed, look as though someone had dropped a heavy rock on its head, an appearance accentuated by the protruding lower jaw.

The flathead catfish is, with the blue and the channel cat, among the biggest of the catfish, with netted specimens of more than 100 lb/45 kg on record. Most caught on rod and reel run to no more than 5 lb/2.3 kg, although in some southern waters anglers who specialize in catching big catfish routinely hook flatheads of 40 or 50 lb/

Flathead catfish

Pylodictis olivaris

DATA

Average weight: 3–5 lb/1.4–2.3 kg.

Fishing tackle: Medium to heavy gear with live bait; setlines and trotlines.

Habitat: Rivers, lakes.

Habits: Waits on bottom with open mouth, into which unwary minnows take cover.

18 or 23 kg. The species' range extends through most rivers of the Mississippi drainage into Mexico.

Flathead catfish are brown, with darker blotches; the tail is rounded or squared off, but never forked. A small flathead may resemble a bullhead, but the band of small teeth on the roof of a flathead's mouth forms a shallow U-shape, while a bullhead has a straight band. In addition, flatheads have fewer than 16 rays in the anal fin, while bullheads have more.

FAMILY ATHERINIDAE

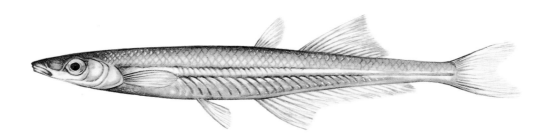

Brook silverside

Labidesthes sicculus

Known as the "skipjack" for the way it launches itself out of the water for short distances, the silverside is a common school fish in big streams and lakes from southern Ontario to Louisiana and Florida.

No bigger than 3 or 4 in/7.5 or 10 cm, the tiny brook silverside is a pencil-thin fish, shiny and in certain lights almost transparent. The divided dorsal fin is set far

DATA

Average length: 2–4 in/5–10 cm.

Habitat: Lakes, rivers, streams.

Habits: Jumps from water when frightened.

back on the body, and the jaws are somewhat elongated, forming a small beak that is distinctive. The anal fin is extremely long, beginning at a point directly below the first dorsal segment, and the tail is forked.

Brook silversides are important forage fish for larger species. When being pursued, a school will erupt from the water's surface, scattering in every direction through the air.

FAMILY GASTEROSTEIDAE

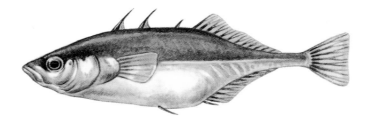

Threespine stickleback

Gasterosteus aculeatus

Generations of school children have learned about the unusual breeding behavior of the sticklebacks. The male of the species industriously weave globular nests of grass and leaves, then entice the females to enter a tunnel through the middle. Inside she lays her eggs, which are immediately fertilized by the male, who guards them and watches after the fry. Even a large bass or sunfish will be routed by the pugnacious male.

Threespine sticklebacks are among the most widespread of fish, found in fresh,

DATA

Average length: 2–4 in/5–10 cm.

Habitat: Streams, ponds, saltwater.

Habits: Male builds grass nest for female.

salt and brackish waters over much of the Northern Hemisphere. In North America, their range includes streams and rivers along the Pacific and northern Atlantic coasts and eastern Canada. The closely related brook stickleback, which usually has five dorsal spines rather than three, is found over much of the northern United States and southern Canada.

Sticklebacks are small fish, at most only 4 in/10 cm long. The basic color is greenish, with darker speckles and blotches.

FAMILY PERCICHTHYIDAE

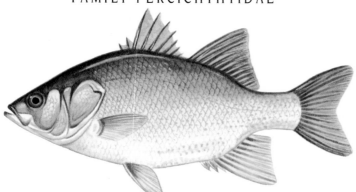

White perch

Morone americana

> **DATA**
>
> **Average weight:** ½–1 lb/225–450 g.
>
> **Fishing tackle:** Ultralight or light gear; small flies, lures, bait.
>
> **Habitat:** Lakes, tidal rivers.
>
> **Habits:** Tolerates wide degree of salinity.

The white perch is one of a number of species of North American fish equally at home in freshwater, saltwater, or salinities in between. Along the Atlantic coast, it is found in bays, tidal creeks, ponds, and rivers, as well as landlocked bodies of water with no access to the ocean. Within historical times it has invaded the eastern Great Lakes, apparently traveling through canals, as several other species of fish, such as the sea lamprey, have done. Intentional transplants also have helped spread the white perch around.

The white perch is a far more benign presence than the lamprey – indeed, it is a favored panfish. While not as large as its close relative, the striped bass, the white perch is entertaining on light tackle, and filleted makes an excellent table fish.

White perch are not true perches, despite the vague resemblance. The body is deep, the back dark (sometimes black), and the sides silvery; there may be faint lateral stripes, especially on smaller specimens. The dorsal fin is divided, and the forward segment is spiny.

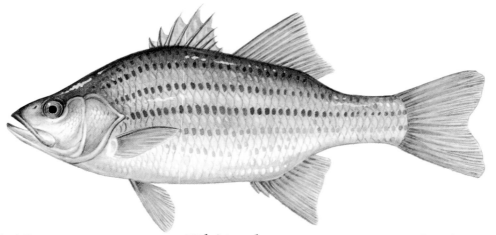

White bass

Morone chrysops

> **DATA**
>
> **Average weight:** 1–2 lb/450–900 g.
>
> **Fishing tackle:** Ultralight or light gear; small lures, bait, especially live minnows.
>
> **Habitat:** Lakes, streams.
>
> **Habits:** Forms large schools.

White bass have attracted a following among sport fishermen out of all proportion to their size. Although lacking the tackle-testing girth of a largemouth bass or northern pike, white bass are scrappy on light tackle, and taste terrific, too. No wonder they are a top game species within their range.

Another of the temperate basses (with the white perch, and yellow and striped basses), the white bass has the same deep, narrow body and high, separate dorsal fins. The color is bright silver, usually with six or seven lateral stripes, which may be complete or broken. The length is usually 15 in/ 38 cm or smaller, with weights of under 2 lb/900 g normal; a 3 or 4 lb/1.4 or 1.8 kg fish is exceptional.

White bass feed on small crustaceans, insects, and small fish, forming large, tight schools that hunt the shallows at dusk and deeper water by day. This species is most common in the center of the United States, from the Great Lakes and St Lawrence south to the Gulf.

Once restricted to the East Coast and its rivers, the anadromous striped bass now exists in landlocked populations as well, growing to tremendous sizes in big reservoirs.

Yellow bass

Morone mississippiensis

DATA

Average weight: 1–2 lb/450–900 g.

Fishing tackle: Ultralight or light gear; small lures and bait, especially minnows.

Habitat: Rivers, lakes.

Habits: Most often caught near bottom.

Very similar to the white bass, the yellow bass has the same general shape, even the same broken lateral stripes, but the body color is usually a bright gold or yellow, rather than silver.

Also like the white bass, the yellow bass is a popular gamefish and even better eating species. However, its range is still more restricted than that of the white bass, inhabiting rivers and lakes from southern Minnesota to parts of the Ohio basin, the south in the Mississippi drainage. Size, food, and life history are much the same as for the white bass (see page 59).

Striped bass

Morone saxatilis

DATA

Average weight: 5–10 lb/2.3–4.5 kg (freshwater).

Fishing tackle: Medium to heavy spinning gear; minnows, jigs or plugs, especially white.

Habitat: Lakes.

Habits: Voracious feeder, attacking schools of forage fish.

The creation of landlocked striped bass fisheries must rank as one of the resounding successes of modern fisheries management, alongside the transplanting of salmon to the Great Lakes. Unlike the salmon, however, the freshwater striped bass have benefited large areas of the eastern United States, especially the South.

Striped bass were originally an anadromous species, found along the Atlantic seaboard, where they are known as "rockfish" and considered one of the top sport species for surf fishing. Little wonder: a large striped bass may weigh 50 lb/23 kg or more, and individuals of more than 120 lb/54 kg have been caught. Within the past 25 years, biologists recognized the potential of stripers as a freshwater gamefish, and planted fingerlings in large reservoirs with an abundance of such forage fish as gizzard shad.

The results have been nothing short of spectacular. In waters where the biggest fish were once 7-lb/3.2-kg largemouths, striped bass of over 40 lb/18 kg are now caught regularly. Even as far north as Pennsylvania's Raystown Lake, striped bass of over 30 lb/14 kg have been taken.

FAMILY CENTRARCHIDAE

Rock bass

Ambloplites rupestris

> **DATA**
>
> **Average weight:** Under ½ lb/225 g.
>
> **Fishing tackle:** Ultralight spinning or fly gear.
>
> **Habitat:** Lakes, rivers, streams.
>
> **Habits:** Prefers rock-strewn areas with moving water.

To youngsters dunking worms in slow-moving creeks and rivers, the rock bass is known – sometimes with affection, sometimes disdain – as "redeyes." It is an aggressive feeder that can save the day when nothing else is biting, or becomes a pest when other gamefish are being sought.

Like many of the group known as panfish, the rock bass has charms that are easily overlooked. Because it does not reach large sizes (1 ft/30 cm is a whopper), it is looked down upon by those seeking smallmouth bass. Yet for its size it fights hard, and on ultralight or fly tackle is as much fun as one of the more "proper" sport species.

Rock bass are variously mottled and spotted, but there are usually distinct lateral stripes, formed by dots on each scale. The eyes are bright red, and the corner of the mouth extends to the center of the eye.

Rock bass are found over a wide area of southern Canada and the northern United States, from New England to the Canadian prairies and south, in a wedge, almost to the Gulf of Mexico. It is fond of cool rivers, streams, and lakes, and like most members of the sunfish family, will feed on any animal small enough to fit into its mouth – usually insects and crustaceans.

Green sunfish

Lepomis cyanellus

> **DATA**
>
> **Average weight:** ½ lb/225 g or less.
>
> **Fishing tackle:** Ultralight; takes small plugs and flies eagerly.
>
> **Habitat:** Lakes, ponds, rivers.
>
> **Habits:** Often takes lures meant for much larger fish.

As with minnows, few anglers bother to differentiate between the many species of sunfish, simply lumping them together as "sunnies," and denigrating them as children's fish. A pity, for sunfish are both fascinating and fun, and the green sunfish is one of the fiercest fighters of the lot.

A green sunfish is built ruggedly, with a chunky body, big head, and ample mouth. The body color is usually greenish, changing to bronze on the lower sides; the opercular flap (a sunfish trademark) is dark with a light edge, and does not extend far beyond the edge of the opercle. The face often carries blue vermiculations. The length is usually 10 in/25 cm or less.

Found in lakes, ponds, and rivers, green sunfish can tolerate warmer, siltier water than many of their relatives. The species is found from the Great Lakes south along the Appalachians to the Gulf, and west as far as Colorado.

Pumpkinseed

Lepomis gibbosus

One of a trio of colorful sunfish (with the longear and redbreast), the pumpkinseed is as whimsical as its name – a jewel of turquoise and orange, plucked from the plainest of waters.

Pumpkinseeds are found over most of the East and Midwest, as well as scattered locations in the West where they have been stocked. In many ponds and lakes it is the commonest sunfish – sometimes the commonest fish – and because it easily over-populates, most waters support thousands

DATA

Average weight: Under ½ lb/225 g.

Fishing tackle: Ultralight or fly gear; bait, small flies.

Habitat: Lakes, ponds.

Habits: Male defends large spawning beds in shallow water.

of scrawny runts, but few big specimens. Where predation keeps the numbers low, however, pumpkinseeds may reach 10 in/ 25 cm, and are great sport on a flyrod.

The opercular flap on the pumpkinseed is dark, with a red or orange spot on the lower corner, and edged with light top and bottom; it does not extend far beyond the opercle. The face is scrawled with powder blue and orange, and the breast is usually orange, especially in males during the early summer spawning season.

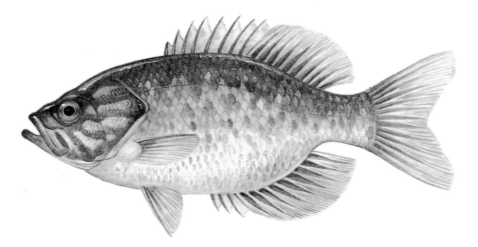

Warmouth

Lepomis gulosus

Often confused with the rock bass, the war-mouth even shares the same nickname – "goggle-eyes" – a reference to its large, reddish eyes. But while the rock bass likes cool, flowing water, the warmouth prefers warmer, still waters in lakes, ponds, and wooded swamps.

A large, aggressive sunfish up to 1 ft/ 30 cm in length, the warmouth is darkly mottled with brown, and has light spots on the dorsal fin and tail. Unlike the rock bass,

DATA

Average weight: Under 1 lb/450 g.

Fishing tackle: Ultralight; often caught accidentally.

Habitat: Lakes, ponds.

Habits: Feeds heavily on crayfish.

the warmouth's anal fin carries spines on the first three rays.

A predator that often specializes in cray-fish, the warmouth also takes a variety of insects, small fish, and crustaceans. It is found from Texas to Minnesota and east to southern New England.

Bluegill

Lepomis macrochirus

DATA

Average weight: ½–1 lb/225–450 g.

North American record: 4 lb 12 oz/ 2.2 kg; Ketona Lake, Alabama, 1950.

Fishing tackle: Ultralight or fly gear; variety of bait and small lures.

Habitat: Lakes, ponds, rivers.

Habits: Males defend large spawning beds.

Not only is the bluegill the most popular panfish – it may well be the most popular game species in North America, if the yardstick is how many are caught, and how many anglers fish for them. Other fish grow bigger and fight harder, but few are found so widely or bite so obligingly.

At a maximum size of 1 ft/30 cm, bluegills are among the bigger of the sunfishes. Old adults are prized, especially in the South where such sizes are not uncommon, and where fishing for "bream" is an honored pastime. A stringer of slabsided bluegills, filleted and cooked, also provide a memorable experience at the table.

Any sunfish with a dark opercular flap may erroneously be called a bluegill. Complicating matters is the bluegill's extremely variable color – even in the same pond they may range from pale yellow-green immatures to old males so dark they appear black. Most have dark vertical bars, and a dark area at the rear base of the dorsal fin. The opercular flap is completely black, and the pectoral fin is long and pointed.

Young bluegills are not shy – hunger forces them to investigate any object that might be remotely edible, and they can be true pests if you are fishing for larger quarry The big oldtimers, though, can be a challenge to catch. They are the ideal flyrod fish, taking both classic wets, nymphs, and dry flies, as well as small marabou streamers and tiny, foam-rubber panfish bugs, usually tied with long, seductively pulsating rubber legs. The traditional bluegill rig, however, includes a plastic bobber, a small hook, and a can of freshly dug earthworms for bait. Even experienced anglers never completely outgrow the thrill of watching the bobber's first, tentative twitches as a bluegill nibbles the bait.

RIGHT Huddled behind a makeshift windscreen, a group of ice-fishermen try their luck for panfish – sunfish, crappies, perch, and bass – which congregate near weed beds and sunken timber.

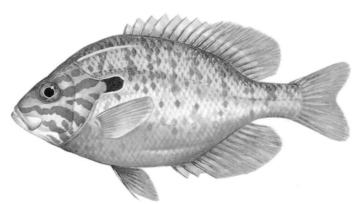

Longear sunfish

Lepomis megalotis

DATA

Average weight: Under ½ lb/225 g.

Fishing tackle: Ultralight or fly gear; variety of bait and lures.

Habitat: Streams, rivers.

Habits: Prefers weedy pools.

The colors of a longear sunfish would seem more at home on a tropical coral reef than weed-choked creeks. An adult fish, especially a male in the summer spawning season, is bright orange, scribbled over liberally with iridescent light blue, particularly strong on the face and dorsal surfaces.

Longear sunfish reach a maximum length of about 10 in/25 cm, although the colder growing seasons of the North reduce the adult size there to about 5 in/13 cm; the average weight is under ½ lb/225 g. The species ranges from southern Ontario and Quebec to the Dakotas and south to Florida, generally west of the Alleghenies.

The similar redbreast sunfish of the Atlantic coastal plain also has a long opercular flap (indeed, even longer than the longear's), but the flap is narrower than the eye, and the body colors are less intense.

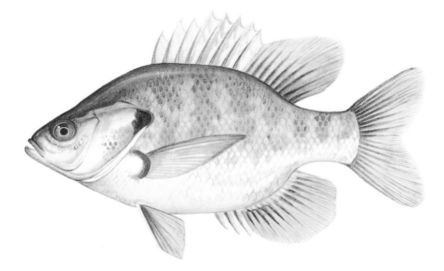

Redear sunfish

Lepomis microlophus

DATA

Average weight: ½–1 lb/225–450 g.

Fishing tackle: Ultralight or fly gear; variety of bait and lures.

Habitat: Lakes, ponds, rivers.

Habits: Eats large numbers of snails.

A drabber version of the pumpkinseed, the redear sunfish lacks its colorful cousin's bluish facial stripes and bright orange accents; the overall tone is yellowish, with dark flecking and mottling on the sides. The breast may be a washed-out shade of yellow or orange, and the opercular flap is black with a reddish tip, without the pumpkinseed's white edging. The pectoral fin is extremely long and graceful.

Originally a southerner, the redear is found naturally from the Carolinas and Illinois south to Florida and Texas, but it has been stocked as far as California. It is a much-sought panfish, known by such local names as yellow bream or shellcracker – the latter name a reference to its fondness for eating snails.

Redear sunfish routinely reach lengths of 10 in/25 cm and weights of 2 lb/900 g or more, which explains their popularity. Like most of the other sunfish, their flesh is firm and sweet, especially lending itself to deep frying.

The smallmouth has few equals as a sport fish. Within its compact, muscular body are reserves of strength continually tapped during the fight, which is usually punctuated with splashy leaps and hard-battled runs. When a smallmouth tail-walks across the surface, tossing water in every direction, the angler's heart stands still.

Aptly known as the "bronzeback," the smallmouth is as attractive as it is tough. Adults take on a brassy sheen, with a reddish eye like a live coal; the scales of the body are often adorned with tiny flecks of gold. Diffuse vertical dark bars may be present; more pronounced dark bars often radiate out from the eye across the face.

Small is a relative term, and while the smallmouth's gape is less than a largemouth bass, it can open wide to suck in food. Crayfish are a preferred dietary item, so much so that to most bass fishermen the two are permanently linked. Smallmouths also take baitfish and plenty of insects, especially larger invertebrates like hellgramites and big caddisflies. On some rivers, mayfly hatches bring the smallmouths to the surface, where they feed with an explosive energy that a trout in similar circumstances never displays.

Smallmouths are classified as warm-water gamefish, but they actually prefer cooler

Smallmouth bass

Micropterus dolomieui

DATA

Average weight: 1–3 lb/450–1400 g.

North American record: 11 lb 15 oz/ 5.4 kg; Dale Hollow Lake, Kentucky, 1955.

Fishing tackle: Light to medium spinning, casting, and fly gear; varity of plugs, spinners, flies, and bait, especially minnows and crayfish.

Habitat: Lakes, rivers.

Habits: Prefers rocky, fast stretches of rivers.

RIGHT Few fish can match the tenacity and spunk of a smallmouth bass, which tends to live in deeper, colder, faster waters than its near relative, the largemouth bass.

waters than largemouth bass. Rivers, large streams, and deep, cold lakes are where they thrive. Originally, this species had a range restricted to the Ohio and St Lawrence river systems, but by the 1800s they were being freighted by train across North America, so that today smallmouths are found as far afield as California and even Hawaii.

The average size ranges from 12 to 18 in/ 30 to 46 cm, and a smallmouth of 5 lb/2.3 kg or bigger is a trophy. In waters where both largemouth and smallmouths occur, confusion is possible. Look at the corner of the closed mouth: in a smallmouth, it comes only to a line through the center of the pupil of the eye; in the largemouth the corner comes well past the rear edge of the orbit.

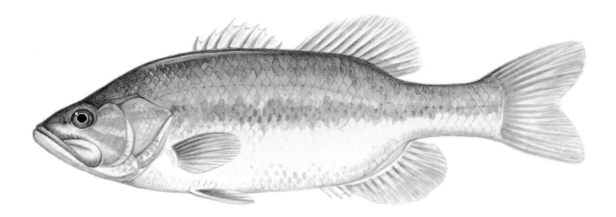

Largemouth bass

Micropterus salmoides

DATA

Average weight: 2–5 lb/900 g–2.3 kg.

North American record: 22 lb 4 oz/ 10.1 kg; Montgomery Lake, Georgia, 1932.

Fishing tackle: Light to medium spinning, casting, and fly gear; wide variety of lures and bait, especially plastic worms and plugs.

Habitat: Lakes, ponds, rivers.

Habits: Lurk near cover, especially floating plant growth.

To call the largemouth "a popular gamefish" is the worst kind of understatement. To millions of anglers, fishing for largemouths borders on an obsession – and little wonder, for this species is big, hard-fighting, and probably as close as the nearest lake or farm pond.

The largemouth has a score of nicknames – bucketmouth, bigmouth, hawg, green trout, green bass. Black bass is a common, if inaccurate, name in many locations. Greenish above and silvery on the belly, the largemouth almost always has a distinct lateral stripe, which in older individuals may be fragmented. The mouth is immense; when closed the corner extends far beyond the edge of the eye, differentiating the fish from spotted and smallmouth bass. When open it is a white cavern, into which may disappear even the most unlikely of food items. Largemouths have been known to eat snakes, ducklings, small mammals, and low-flying songbirds, as well as more normal fare like frogs, fish, salamanders, and insects.

Largemouth bass show a preference for quiet water. In rivers they are found in the slowest and weediest of pools, leaving the faster water to smallmouths, but they are most at home in lakes, ponds, marshes, and swamps – and the more cover, the better. Bass fishermen long ago recognized the importance of "structure," the catch-all term for sunken logs, rock piles, weed beds, drop-offs, and other hiding places. Largemouths often patrol their home range looking for food, but much of the time they spend waiting quietly beneath lily pads or next to flooded timber, hoping for a meal to happen by.

The greatest number of largemouths are caught on casting or spinning tackle, with such lures as plastic worms, spinnerbaits, and pork rinds – all bass specialities. The largest, however, are usually taken on live bait, such as big golden shiners. Fly-fishermen, who have long extolled the virtues of trout and smallmouths, are rediscovering the thrill of hooking a 6- or 7-lb/2.7- or 3.2-kg largemouth on light tackle; deer-hair bugs and fur-strip streamers are excellent choices.

The biggest largemouths, in excess of 12 lb/5.4 kg, come from the South, where year-round growing seasons allow them to reach the maximum size. The world record, at 22 lb 4 oz/10.1 kg, came from Georgia, but many experts suspect bigger bass lurk in California, where the giant Florida subspecies has been widely stocked.

Largemouth bass like their quarters crowded – plenty of lilypads, sunken logs, or other cover nearby, from which they can launch a lightning ambush if food should come by.

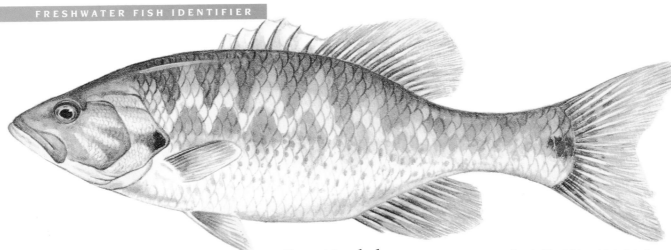

Spotted bass

Micropterus punctulatus

DATA

Average weight: 1–2 lb/450–900 g.

North American record: 8 lb 15 oz/ 4.1 kg; Lewis Smith Lake, Alabama, 1978.

Fishing tackle: Same as for other bass.

Habitat: Lakes, rivers, streams.

Habits: In rivers, prefers calmer waters than smallmouth.

To the casual observer, the spotted bass lies somewhere between a smallmouth and a largemouth. Like a smallmouth, the spotted bass has a mouth that does not extend past the middle of the eye, it has scales on the base of the dorsal and ventral fins, and a dual dorsal fin joined in the middle. Like the largemouth, it has a dark lateral stripe, but has none of the small-mouth's vertical barring.

Not a hybrid, as once thought, the spotted bass is a species in its own right, occupying a range that extends from the central states to the Gulf, within which it is found in lakes, rivers, and creeks. The best field mark for the spotted bass are the distinct rows of dark spots below the lateral line, which form thin stripes running from the pectoral fin to the tail.

Spotted bass do not grow as big as large-mouths, or even smallmouths; 5 lb/2.3 kg is the top weight. Nevertheless, they are an excellent sport fish, and are an important game species within their range.

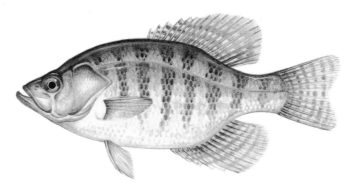

White crappie

Pomoxis annularis

DATA

Average weight: ½–1 lb/225–450 g.

North American record: 5 lb 3 oz/2.4 kg; Enid Dam, Mississippi, 1957.

Fishing tackle: Ultralight spinning gear; jigs, spinners, small plugs, live minnows.

Habitat: Lakes, rivers.

Habits: Form large schools.

Aside from the larger bass, the two species of crappies may rank first among the sunfish in the amount of fish in the diet. Anglers who specialize in catching the biggest "slab" crappies know that a minnow imita-tion, particularly a marabou jig, is usually the most effective lure.

Crappies have an elegance of design missing in many of the sunfish. The dorsal and anal fins are large and almost mirror images of each other, and the head is somewhat lengthened into a pug-nosed snout. The white crappie is pale silver with faint, vertical bars on the sides, although the bars may be indistinct in some indi-viduals. It is almost identical to the black crappie, which lacks the barring and has seven or eight dorsal spines, rather than the six possessed by the white crappie.

White crappies are lake and large-river inhabitants, tolerant of warmer, siltier water than black crappies. They form dense schools of even-age fish, and provide terrific fishing, especially in spring when they move into shallow water to spawn. Most are under 1 ft/30 cm long and 1 lb/450 g in weight, although 3- or 4-lb/1.4- or 1.8-kg specimens are not unheard of.

The white crappie is found naturally over most of eastern North America, south of the Great Lakes, and has been stocked in many parts of the West.

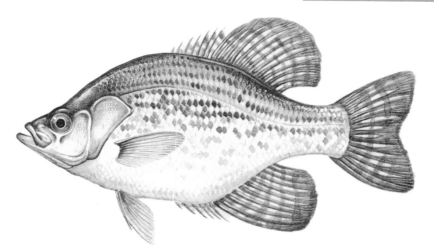

Black crappie

Pomoxis nigromaculatus

DATA

Average weight: 1–2 lb/450–900 g.

North American record: 4 lb 8 oz/2 kg; Kerr Dam, Virginia, 1981.

Fishing tackle: Ultralight spinning gear; jigs, small plugs, live minnows.

Habitat: Lakes.

Habits: Often found near submerged weed beds.

Seemingly a carbon copy of the white crappie, the black is covered with a fine checkerboard of dark scales, giving it the regional name "calico bass."

Like the white, the black crappie is a fine gamefish, well suited to ultralight tackle with jigs, live minnows, or tiny, sinking plugs. It, too, is a schooling fish, so that when an angler catches one, it is a good bet that there are plenty more nearby. The black crappie is fussier about its habitat, though, doing best in cooler, clear lakes, especially those with a heavy growth of aquatic vegetation.

By natural occurrence or stocking, the black crappie is found in almost every part of temperate North America. Where food is abundant, it may reach a weight of 5 lb/2.3 kg or more, although the average black crappie is under 1 ft/30 cm long, and weighs 1 to 2 lb/450 to 900 g.

BELOW Often called "calicos," black crappies are terrific sport on light tackle; the closely related white crappie is similar, but has dark vertical bars rather than scattered black flecking.

FAMILY PERCIDAE

Rainbow darter

Etheostoma caeruleum

DATA

Average length: 1–3 in/2.5–7.5 cm.

Habitat: Lakes, streams, rivers.

Habits: Bottom-dweller; male defends nest in gravel bed.

There are more than 120 species of darters, all of them east of the Rockies, and many restricted to single streams or rivers. All are small bottom-dwellers that hop about on their pectoral fins, swimming with a quick, darting motion only when necessary. They are also the most colorful group in freshwater, few more so than the rainbow darter.

Males in spring spawning colors are as breathtaking as any woodland bird. The tail, dorsal, and anal fins are red, with edgings of blue and white; the throat has a red slash, and the body is bluish, with orange flecks overlayed against dark, vertical bars. As the male hops about the bottom of the stream or lake, it flares its fins aggressively at intruders – even at a curious human in swim mask and snorkel. Come too close, and the brilliant mite will attack the glass in front of your face.

Rainbow darters grow to 3 in/7.5 cm, and are found in cold waters from Arkansas north through the Mississippi and Ohio valleys to southeastern Canada.

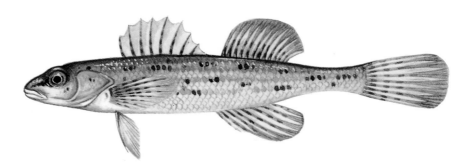

Johnny darter

Etheostoma nigrum

DATA

Average length: 1–2 in/2.5–5 cm.

Habitat: Streams, rivers.

Habits: Feeds on minute invertebrates.

Common in streams and rivers over much of eastern North America, the Johnny darter is a rather drab member of this normally colorful family. It is the color of water-polished gravel, buffy with darker, W-shaped blotches that merge on spawning males to form a heavier tone.

The Johnny darter is slim, with a drooping mouth and mottled fins; a large specimen is 3 in/7.5 cm long, and most are no more than an 1 in/2.5 cm. Despite its size and retiring habits (it is a bottom-dweller, like all darters), it plays an important role in the diet of gamefish like trout, and the Muddler minnow, one of the most famous trout flies, is an accurate imitation of a darter.

Johnny darters show a tolerance for slightly warmer, more turbid water than most other darters, although even in such streams they will be found in rocky riffles, where they can dart beneath a stone should danger threaten.

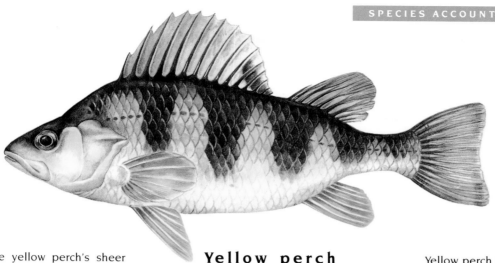

Yellow perch

Perca flavascens

DATA

Average weight: 1 lb/450 g or less.

North American record: 4 lb 3 oz/1.9 kg; Bordentown, New Jersey, 1865.

Fishing tackle: Light gear; spinners, jigs, live bait.

Habitat: Lakes, ponds, rivers.

Habits: Very important forage species for larger gamefish.

In many lakes, the yellow perch's sheer fecundity works against it. Overpopulation renders most of the perch stunted and accomplished pests, capable of stealing the bait meant for bigger fish.

Where there are predators like northern pike to hold the population in check, however, the yellow perch can grow to a weight of several pounds (kilogram), making it a worthy quarry in its own right. Even more important to many anglers, though, is how the perch tastes – arguably one of the finest eating fish in North America. A commercial fishery on the Great Lakes has long focused on this delectable species.

Yellow perch are hard to mistake for any other fish. Their bright gold body color is marked with five to eight dark, vertical bars, and the ventral fins are usually a rich orange. The average size for a mature perch is 12 to 15 in/30 to 38 cm, with weights of 2 lb/900 g not unusual; they rarely grow bigger, although a monster of 4½ lb/2 kg was caught in the 1800s in New Jersey.

Found in lakes, ponds, and rivers, the yellow perch ranges from the Atlantic coastal plain to northern Quebec, then west to the Plains and the Northwest Territories. It has been stocked far beyond its original range, as well.

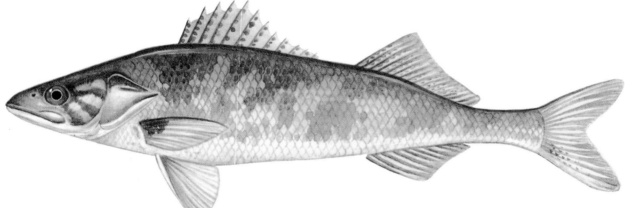

Sauger

Stizostedion canadense

DATA

Average weight: 3–5 lb/1.4–2.3 kg.

Fishing tackle: Medium gear; plugs, spinners, jigs, and live bait, especially minnows.

Habitat: Lakes, rivers.

Habits: Prefers larger waters than walleyes.

A lookalike for the better-known walleye, the sauger is found only in the largest of lakes and rivers from Quebec to Saskatchewan, south through the Mississippi system to the central United States.

For many years, anglers made no attempt to separate sauger from walleye, since the two are so similar in appearance. Both are long and slim, with large, tooth-studded mouths and double dorsal fins, the first spiny. Both are brassy brown, but while the walleye has diffuse blotches, the sauger's markings usually form three or four saddles over the back. The sauger's mouth is larger, with the corner extending past the rear of the eye, rather than just to the middle as in the walleye. Also, the sauger lacks the walleye's white tip to the lower tail lobe.

The biggest saugers are considerably smaller than the biggest walleyes (a maximum of 9 lb/4.1 kg, versus the walleye's 25 lb/11 kg), but the average size of 3 to 5 lb/1.4 to 2.3 kg is comparable in both species. Sauger make long-distance migrations in rivers, and are an increasingly important gamefish in many areas.

Small but tasty, yellow perch are among the most popular of panfish, even though they rarely grow longer than 10 or 12 in/25 or 30 cm.

Walleye

Stizostedion vitreum

DATA

Average weight: 3–5 lb/1.4–2.3 kg.

North American record: 25 lb/11.3 kg; Old Hickery Lake, Tennessee, 1960.

Fishing tackle: Light to medium gear; spinners, jigs, plugs, and live bait, especially minnows.

Habitat: Lakes, rivers, streams.

Habits: Feeds at night in shallow water.

Walleye rank with largemouth bass and the various trout as the most popular of freshwater gamefish. Capable of putting up a dogged, if unimaginative, fight, the walleye really shines in the pan, for its sweet flesh is perhaps the best the North American continent has to offer.

The biggest of the true perches, walleyes usually average between 2 and 8 lb/900 g and 3.6 kg, but may be caught much larger, with trophy fish in excess of 20 lb/9 kg not unusual in some waters. The odd name comes from the fish's equally odd eyes, which have a glassy, highly reflective pupil; take a flash picture of a stringer of walleyes, and in the finished photograph the eyes all will be glowing with a ghostly white reflection. The eye structure is an adaptation for the deep water in which walleyes are usually found, where light is scarce. After dark the schools will move into shallow water, chasing down baitfish, crayfish, and insects.

Walleyes like big water – lakes, rivers, and large, deep streams, especially those with cool, silt-free water and a bottom of gravel or rock. In spring usually just after ice-out, the walleyes make spawning runs from lakes into tributary rivers; in larger lakes the walleyes spawn on gravel-strewn shoals. Most states and provinces protect the walleyes during spawning, with the season opener – and best fishing of the year – coming just after the fish move off the breeding grounds, before they return to deep water.

The walleye resembles the sauger to a great degree, but the smaller mouth and the white tip to the lower tail lobe are usually diagnostic.

One of the most shameful chapters of North American fisheries management – or mismanagement – was the apparent extinction of the blue pike, a subspecies of the walleye found only in Lake Erie. Once one of the most important commercial species in the region, it was overfished in the middle of the 20th century, and has not been seen in years.

RIGHT Walleyes can be found in large, cool lakes, rivers, and even big streams, especially during the spring spawning run.

FAMILY SCIAENIDAE

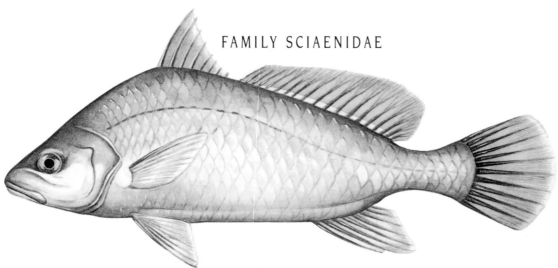

Freshwater drum

Aplodinotus grunniens

DATA

Average weight: 1–5 lb/450 g–2.3 kg.

Fishing tackle: Often takes lures meant for gamefish.

Habitat: Lakes, rivers.

Habits: Makes noticeable "drumming" noise.

The renegade of an otherwise saltwater family, the freshwater drum is cousin to such oceanic luminaries as the red drum, seatrout, and weakfish. Found from the Plains to the western slopes of the Appalachians, the drum's range encompasses rivers and lakes as far north as James Bay, and as far south as Guatemala.

A humpbacked, heavy-bodied fish, the drum's long, joined dorsal fins, rounded tail, large underslung mouth, and two anal fin spines separate it from other fish in its range. The color is dull silver, a bit darker above and lighter below, but otherwise unremarkable.

What is remarkable about the drum is the fish's habit of vibrating the muscles around its air bladder, which serves as a resonating chamber, magnifying the sound to a low rumble. A bottom-dweller, the drum feeds primarily on mollusks, although insects, crustaceans, and small fish are also taken. The average size is under 5 lb/2.3 kg, although commercially netted drums of more than 50 lb/23 kg have been reported.

FAMILY COTTIDAE

Mottled sculpin

Cottus bairdi

DATA

Average length: 4–6 in/10–15 cm.

Habitat: Rivers, streams.

Habits: Bottom-dweller.

The mottled sculpin is a fish that has raised the art of camouflage to new levels. Squat and stone-like to begin with, the sculpin is clad in a jumble of brown and black blotches that make it impossible to see when resting among the rocks of a stream bottom, its preferred habitat.

Sculpins bear a superficial resemblance to darters, with their large pectoral fins and long, double dorsal fins, but there is no close kinship. The sculpin's head is wide and flattened, accounting for the old name of "miller's thumb," a reference to the grotes-quely flattened thumb a man gets after years of pressing against a millstone.

Mottled sculpins are found in rivers and streams, as well as some lakes, from arctic Quebec to the southern Appalachians and west to the Plains. A disjunct population is also found in many parts of the West, where this and related species are known as bullheads. The mottled sculpin is a favored food of large trout, especially trophy browns, and many of the most successful streamers incorporate the sculpin's wide head and bottom-hugging habits.

Glossary

Adipose fin – Small, fleshy fin, posterior to dorsal fins; characteristic of trout, smelt, and catfish.

Anadromous – Fish, such as salmon, that spawns in freshwater but matures in saltwater.

Anal fin – Fin posterior to anus on ventral surface of body.

Anal spine – Stiff rays in anterior of anal fin.

Anterior – Pertaining to front or forward portion; opposite of posterior.

Axillary process – Small scale or ridge jutting out at base of pelvic fins.

Branchiostegal rays – Thin bones that support gill membrane; visible under fish's throat.

Catadromous – Fish, such as eel, that spawns in saltwater but matures in freshwater.

Caudal fin – Tail membrane.

Caudal peduncle – Slender portion of posterior body that serves as anchor for the caudal fin.

Compressed – Body shape; very narrow seen head-on, very deep in profile.

Dorsal – Pertaining to top or upper surfaces; opposite of ventral.

Dorsal fin – One or two large fins along median of back; may be spiny, in part.

Dorsal spine – Stiff, pointed ray in dorsal fin, usually in anterior portion.

Freestone – Stream flowing over non-limestone substrata; relatively sterile.

Ganoid scales – Primitive, diamond-shaped scales that do not overlap; found in gars.

Gill rakers – Specialized, fingerlike protuberances from gill arches; serve as plankton collectors in some species, such as shad.

Hard rays – Soft rays that have fused to form a spine; found in catfish and carp.

Inferior mouth – Downturned mouth.

Kype – Hooked jaw; found in many species of salmon.

Lateral line – String of sensory pores running the length of many fish.

Limestone creek – Stream flowing over limestone or similar substrata; very rich in plant and animal life.

Opercle – Posterior portion of gill flap.

Opercular flap – Posterior extension of opercle.

Pectoral fin – Fin found on side of body just posterior of opercle.

Pelvic fin – Paired fins just anterior of anus.

Posterior – Pertaining to rear portion; opposite of anterior.

Ray – Structures that support fins; may be soft or hard.

Soft ray – Flexible fin support; soft ray count often important identification feature.

Spine – Sharply pointed ray, often in anterior portions of dorsal and anal fins.

Terminal mouth – Mouth set at roughly the anterior of the head; not downturned.

Ventral – Pertaining to lower surfaces or underside; opposite of dorsal.

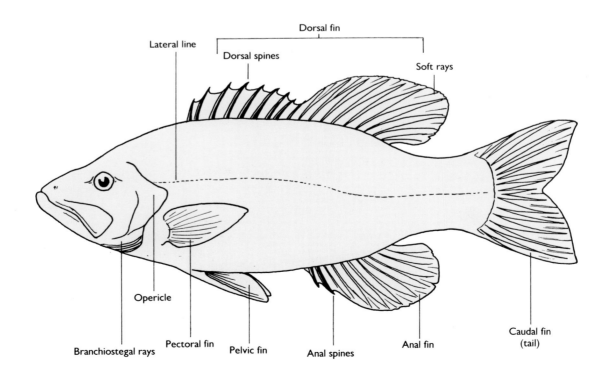

Index

Acknowledgments

The Publishers would like to thank **Andrew Tewson**, a student of **The School of Illustration, Bournemouth and Poole College of Art and Design**, for the specially commissioned illustrations featured in this book.

They would also like to thank the following, for supplying photographs: © **Tom Fegely** pages 9, 10, 23, 27, 36–37, 65, 69, 71, 74–75; © **Tom Huggler** pages 6, 29, 67; © **Scott Weidensaul** pages 7, 8, 11, 32; © 1989 **Joe Workosky** pages 14, 33, 40, 60–61, 76.